AFRICAN AMERICAN ACHIEVERS
HIGH-INTEREST NONFICTION

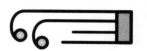

BY
KATHRYN WHEELER

CARSON-DELLOSA PUBLISHING COMPANY, INC.
GREENSBORO, NORTH CAROLINA

CREDITS

Editor: Carrie Fox
Layout Design: Lori Jackson
Inside Illustrations: Stefano Giorgi
Cover Design: Peggy Jackson
Cover Illustration: Tara Tavonatti

This book has been correlated to state, national, and Canadian provincial standards. Visit *www.carsondellosa.com* to search for and view its correlations to your standards.

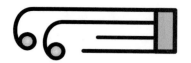 # TABLE OF CONTENTS

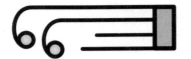 

INTRODUCTION

Invite students to experience the thrill of reading with the historical biographies in *African American Achievers: High-Interest Nonfiction.*

The passages in this book are appropriate for students in the intermediate grades. Among these grade levels, and even within individual classrooms, you will find learners at different reading levels. When presenting students with a new text, there is always the danger of either frustrating struggling readers or boring those students who have jumped ahead. To help all of these students maintain interest and find success in their reading assignments, this book presents each passage at two different reading levels.

Also included with each passage is a set of comprehension questions that applies to both versions of the story and a bonus activity. The questions test students' skills in determining main idea, reading for details, sequencing, using context clues, and drawing conclusions. The bonus activity is a writing extension that reinforces reasoning skills and encourages students to connect prior knowledge with the text.

An assessment grid at the back of the book makes it easy to see which reading comprehension skills each student has mastered.

An icon in the lower right or left corner of each passage designates the reading level.

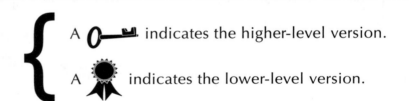

Use the rubric below to help you assess students' writing after they have completed the bonus writing extension following each passage.

	NOVICE	EMERGING	INDEPENDENT	DISTINGUISHED
TOPIC	Did not stay on topic	Stayed on topic for most of the paragraph	Stayed on topic	Stayed on topic with elaboration
ORGANIZATION	Not organized	Organized	Well organized	Outstanding organization
WRITTEN EXPRESSION	Hard to understand	Easier to understand	Easy to understand	Well written, elaborated

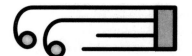 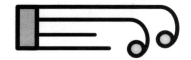

BENJAMIN BANNEKER
(1731–1806)

The young man bent over the pocket watch. In the 1700s, a pocket watch was a rare and valuable thing. Clocks and watches were not made in the colonies of America. The young man borrowed this watch from a wealthy neighbor. But, he did not want to show it off or use it—he wanted to take it apart! Piece by piece, the 21 year old took apart the precious watch. Carefully, he made a drawing of each tiny gear and component. Then, he put the whole watch together again.

Benjamin Banneker was the son of a former slave. He lived as a free man in Maryland. Even though Benjamin had only gone to school for a short time, he was full of curiosity. He loved the fascinating pieces of the watch, so he started to make large-sized copies of the gears. He carved these pieces out of wood. He added **chimes** to ring for each hour. When it was done, his hand-carved clock was the first chiming clock ever made in America. Even though the wooden parts wore down over time, the clock worked perfectly for 50 years.

After his parents died, Benjamin ran their farm. He also repaired watches and clocks. Thanks to his work on the pocket watch, he knew how to fix them.

What else did Benjamin find interesting? He liked to study the stars. In one of the fields on his farm, Benjamin built a "work cabin." The cabin had a skylight cut in the roof. He looked at the stars through this hole in the roof and made charts of the sky. Then, he wrote and published an almanac, a book that showed when the moon would be full and when people should plant crops.

In 1791, Benjamin was given a new job. He was asked to help survey, or map out, the new city of Washington, D.C., with a man named Andrew Ellicott. A Frenchman named Pierre L'Enfant was going to design the new city—the roads, government buildings, and parks. L'Enfant had a bad temper and was unreliable. He was fired. The government had paid for his plans, but L'Enfant took the plans with him when he left. Many people believe that Benjamin came to the rescue. They say that he helped Ellicott remember every detail of the plans and drew them all from memory! The work on Washington, D.C., went on, partially thanks to Benjamin Banneker.

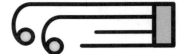
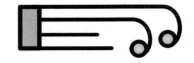

BENJAMIN BANNEKER
(1731–1806)

The young man bent over the watch. In the 1700s, a watch was a rare and valuable thing. Clocks and watches were not made in the colonies of America. The young man borrowed this watch from a wealthy neighbor. But, he did not want to show it off. He did not want to use it. He wanted to take it apart! The 21 year old took apart the watch piece by piece. He made a drawing of each tiny gear and part. Then, he put the whole watch back together again.

Benjamin Banneker was the son of a freed slave. He lived in Maryland. Banneker only went to school for a short time. But, he was interested in everything around him. He loved the watch. He started to make big copies of the gears. He carved these pieces out of wood. He added **chimes**. They rang for each hour. When it was done, his hand-carved clock was the first clock of its kind made in America. The wooden parts wore down over time, but the clock worked perfectly for 50 years.

After Benjamin's parents died, he ran their farm. He also repaired watches and clocks. Thanks to his neighbor's watch, he knew how to fix them.

What else did Benjamin find interesting? He liked the stars. In one of the fields on his farm, Benjamin built a "work cabin." The cabin had a skylight cut in the roof. He looked at the stars through this hole in the roof. He made charts of the sky. He wrote and published an almanac. This was a book that showed when the moon would be full and when people should plant crops.

In 1791, Benjamin was given a new job. He was asked to help a man named Andrew Ellicott map out the new city of Washington, D.C. A man from France named Pierre L'Enfant planned the roads, buildings, and parks for the city. L'Enfant had a bad temper. He was fired. The government had paid for his plans. But, L'Enfant took the plans with him when he left. Many people think that Benjamin came to the rescue. They say that he helped Ellicott draw all of the plans from memory. The work on Washington, D.C., went on, in part thanks to Benjamin Banneker.

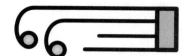

BENJAMIN BANNEKER
(1731–1806)

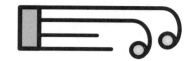

1. Choose a good title for this story.

   A. Watching the Stars

   B. An Interesting Life

   C. Looking at Maps

   D. From Clocks to the Capital

2. What does the word **chimes** mean in the story?

   A. the part of a clock that ticks

   B. the parts of a clock that hold the gears together

   C. the part of a clock that rings for each hour

   D. the part of a clock that points to each hour

3. Number the following events in the order they happened.

   ____ Benjamin is asked to help plan the city of Washington, D.C.

   ____ Benjamin gets a farm after his parents die.

   ____ Benjamin takes apart his neighbor's pocket watch.

   ____ Benjamin draws the plans for Washington, D.C., from memory.

   ____ Benjamin starts to study the stars.

4. Answer the following questions.

   • Where did Benjamin Banneker live as a child?

   _____

   • What did Benjamin build after he took apart the watch?

   _____

   • Why did Benjamin build his "work cabin"?

   _____

   _____

   • Who was Pierre L'Enfant?

   _____

   _____

5. Why do you think that Benjamin was asked to help map the new city of Washington, D.C.?

   A. He was a good farmer.

   B. He was good at details, and he knew how to make maps of the stars.

   C. He knew how to fix clocks and pocket watches.

   D. He was a free man.

BONUS: Have you ever wanted to take apart a machine to see how it works? What do you think would happen if you tried it? Write a story pretending that you took apart a machine at your house. Tell about what happens.

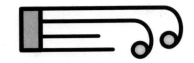

ELIZABETH FREEMAN
(1742–1829)

Colonel John Ashley had a fine home in Sheffield, Massachusetts. He often had guests who talked about the new Bill of Rights and the new state constitution. The people who sat around the table were not the only ones listening, though. Also listening to these new ideas about freedom was a slave who **waited on** the table. She was called Mum Bett.

Mum Bett heard the guests say that all people in the state "were free and equal." She decided that meant her, too—even though she was black. She decided she wanted to be free and find a new home.

The Ashley house was not a comfortable place for slaves to live. Mrs. Ashley once tried to hit Mum Bett's sister with a hot coal shovel. Mum Bett put herself in front of her sister and was hit and burned instead. One day, Mum Bett left the house, knowing that she would never go back.

Instead, she went to see a lawyer named Theodore Sedgwick. She asked him to help her go to court to win her freedom. Sedgwick helped her by speaking for her in court. He argued the same point that Mum Bett had made to him. If the state law said that everyone in the state was free, didn't that mean Mum Bett was free, too? The court agreed that it did. A few years later, Massachusetts ended slavery in the state, thanks to Mum Bett and her case.

Mum Bett took a new name after the court case: Elizabeth Freeman. It was a name that showed how proud she was to be free. She went to work for the Sedgwick family as a paid housekeeper. She got married and had children who grew up in the state that their own mother helped to make free for everybody.

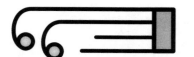 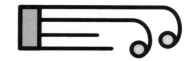

ELIZABETH FREEMAN
(1742–1829)

Colonel John Ashley had a big home in Sheffield, Massachusetts. He had guests at his home. They talked about the new Bill of Rights and new state laws. The people who sat around the table were not the only ones listening, though. A slave who **waited on** the table listened, too. She heard the new ideas about freedom. She was called Mum Bett.

Mum Bett heard the guests say that all people in the state "were free and equal." She thought that meant her, too—even though she was black. She wanted to be free and find a new home.

The Ashley house was not a good place for slaves to live. Mrs. Ashley once tried to hit Mum Bett's sister with a hot coal shovel. Mum Bett put herself in front of her sister. She was hit and burned instead. One day, Mum Bett left the house. She never went back.

Mum Bett went to see a lawyer. His name was Theodore Sedgwick. She asked him to help her go to court. She wanted to win her freedom. Sedgwick helped her. He used the same point that Mum Bett had made to him. If the state law said that everyone in the state was free, didn't that mean Mum Bett was free, too? The court said that it did. A few years later, Massachusetts ended slavery in the state. This was thanks to Mum Bett and her case.

Mum Bett took a new name after the court case: Elizabeth Freeman. It was a name that showed how proud she was to be free. She went to work for the Sedgwick family. They paid her for her work. She got married and had children. Her children grew up in the state that their mother helped to make free for everybody.

ELIZABETH FREEMAN
(1742–1829)

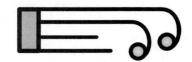

1. The fifth (last) paragraph is mainly about:

   A. Mum Bett's court case.

   B. Mum Bett's life after winning her freedom.

   C. Mum Bett's sister.

   D. Mum Bett's life with the Ashley family.

2. What do the words **waited on** mean in the story?

   A. lingered

   B. expected

   C. served

   D. rested

3. Number the following events in the order they happened.

   _____ Mum Bett is a slave in the house of John Ashley.

   _____ Elizabeth Freeman has children.

   _____ Mum Bett changes her name to Elizabeth Freeman.

   _____ Mum Bett wins her case in court.

   _____ Mum Bett goes to talk to Theodore Sedgwick about her idea.

4. Answer the following questions.

   • Who was Theodore Sedgwick?

   _____

   • Where did Mum Bett live?

   _____

   • How did Mum Bett's court case make a big change in the state?

   _____

   _____

   • Why did Mum Bett change her name?

   _____

5. What first made Mum Bett think that she could win her freedom in court?

   A. Theodore Sedgwick said that he would take her case to court.

   B. Mrs. Ashley burned her.

   C. She knew she could be paid for her work and earn her own living.

   D. She heard talk about laws that said everyone in the state was free.

BONUS: Have you ever felt something happened to you that was not right? Write about that time.

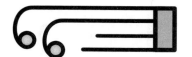

PHILLIS WHEATLEY
(1753?–1784)

The little girl in the market looked ill and cold. She was only seven years old and was frightened and alone. A woman named Susannah Wheatley saw the child who was being sold as a slave. John and Susannah Wheatley bought her. They named the little girl Phillis after the slave ship that carried the stolen girl from Africa to Boston, Massachusetts.

Mrs. Wheatley was kind to little Phillis. She asked her daughter Mary to teach Phillis English. In a little more than a year, Phillis learned how to read and write in English. The little girl was very smart, and soon she knew more than her teacher! Phillis learned how to read Latin and Greek. She wrote her first poem when she was only 13 years old.

It was lucky for Phillis that Mrs. Wheatley was not like other slave owners. Mrs. Wheatley treated Phillis more like one of her children than a servant, which meant that Phillis had time to read, write, and think.

When Phillis was only 14 years old, she published a poem in a Newport, Rhode Island, newspaper. People were amazed by the beauty of the poem. Phillis composed many poems. The Wheatleys told Phillis that she should publish a book of her poems. A friend in London, England, would help Phillis get the book printed.

Phillis sailed to London. She became well-known in London society and met many famous people, including Benjamin Franklin. People **prized** her poems. But, Phillis left her admirers quickly when she found out that Mrs. Wheatley was ill. Phillis crossed the ocean again to Boston to be with her. Before Mrs. Wheatley died, she freed Phillis.

Phillis married John Peters, another freed slave. She kept writing and worked on another book. Sadly, Phillis died before the book could be published, and now, it is lost. But, what will never be lost is Phillis Wheatley's accomplishment. She was the first African American author to publish a book of poems.

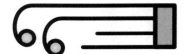

PHILLIS WHEATLEY
(1753?–1784)

The little girl in the market looked sick and cold. She was only seven years old. She was scared and alone. A woman named Susannah Wheatley saw the child. The little girl was being sold as a slave. John and Susannah Wheatley bought her. They named the little girl Phillis. That was the name of the slave ship that carried the stolen girl from Africa to Boston, Massachusetts.

Mrs. Wheatley was kind to little Phillis. She asked her daughter Mary to teach Phillis English. In a little more than a year, Phillis learned how to read and write in English. The little girl was very smart. Soon, she knew more than her teacher! Phillis learned how to read Latin and Greek. She wrote her first poem when she was 13 years old.

Phillis was lucky. Mrs. Wheatley was not like other slave owners. Mrs. Wheatley treated Phillis like one of her children. Phillis had time to read, write, and think.

Phillis had a poem printed in a Newport, Rhode Island, newspaper. She was only 14 years old. People thought the poem was beautiful. Phillis wrote many poems. The Wheatleys told Phillis that she should sell a book of her poems. A friend in London, England, would help Phillis get the book printed.

Phillis went to London. She became well-known there. She met many famous people, like Benjamin Franklin. People **prized** her poems. But, Phillis had to leave quickly. She found out that Mrs. Wheatley was sick. Phillis went back to Boston to be with her. Mrs. Wheatley freed Phillis before she died.

Phillis married a man named John Peters. He was also a freed slave. She kept writing. She worked on another book. Sadly, Phillis died before the book could be printed. Now, the book is lost. But, what will never be lost is Phillis Wheatley's accomplishment. She was the first African American author to get a book of poems printed.

PHILLIS WHEATLEY
(1753?–1784)

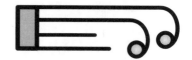

1. This story mainly tells about:

   A. a girl who was sold into slavery and then became a poet.

   B. a slave who went to London.

   C. a slave who was sold when she was seven.

   D. a girl who married another freed slave.

2. What does the word **prized** mean in the story?

   A. won

   B. printed

   C. disliked

   D. valued

3. Number the following events in the order they happened.

   ____ Phillis Wheatley marries John Peters.

   ____ Phillis works on her second book of poems.

   ____ Phillis learns Latin and Greek.

   ____ Phillis Wheatley is freed.

   ____ Phillis meets Benjamin Franklin.

BONUS: Write a story about someone finding Phillis Wheatley's lost book of poems. Where was the book found? What do the poems say?

4. Answer the following questions.

   • Who was Susannah Wheatley?

   _____

   _____

   • Why was Phillis Wheatley luckier than many slaves?

   _____

   _____

   • Where did the name "Phillis" come from?

   _____

   _____

   • What was Phillis Wheatley's biggest accomplishment?

   _____

   _____

5. Why do you think that it was unusual for Phillis to go London?

   A. She did not like to travel on ships.

   B. Slaves were not usually allowed to go on trips.

   C. She did not have a place to stay when she got to London.

   D. Women did not usually go to London.

DAVID WALKER
(1785?–1830)

David Walker was born to a free mother. The law said that made him free, too. But, David's father was a slave. The family lived in North Carolina, where there were big plantations and many slaves. The young boy grew up hating the very idea of slavery.

When David grew up, he left the South, but he was not turning his back on the slaves he had known. Instead, he moved to Boston, Massachusetts, so that he could fight for their freedom.

David started to work for an African American newspaper. In 1829, he wrote an article for the newspaper about the evils of slavery. David wrote two more long articles. He put the articles into a book that was called *Walker's Appeal*. In the *Appeal*, David told slaves that they should rise up against their masters. He told them that they had the right to be free.

By the time David wrote his book, he owned a store that sold used clothing to sailors and poor people. He used this store to **smuggle** copies of his book into the South so that slaves could read it. He sewed copies of the book into pieces of clothing. People wore the clothing until they got to the South. Then, they gave the hidden books to slaves.

Many people were afraid of David's strong words. Some states passed laws that made it against the law for slaves to read so that they could not read David's book. One group of people offered a reward of $10,000 to anyone who could capture David and bring him to the South. David's friends were frightened for him. They begged him to go to Canada where slavery was illegal and he would be safe, but David refused. He said that he would be willing to die to make slaves free.

Not long after that, David Walker was found dead in his home. He may have died of tuberculosis, a disease that affects the lungs. His work for slaves ended in one way, but his powerful words live on.

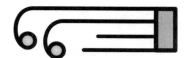
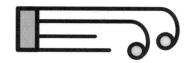

DAVID WALKER
(1785?–1830)

David Walker was born to a free mother. The law said that made him free, too. But, David's father was a slave. The family lived in North Carolina, where there were big plantations and many slaves. The young boy grew up hating slavery.

When David grew up, he left the South, but he was not turning his back on the slaves he had known. Instead, he moved to Boston, Massachusetts, to fight for their freedom.

David went to work for an African American newspaper. He wrote his first newspaper story in 1829. The story told about the hard lives of slaves. David wrote two more long articles. He put his writing into a book. It was called *Walker's Appeal*. In his book, David told slaves to rise up against their masters. He told them that they had the right to be free.

By this time, David had a store that sold used clothing. The store sold clothes to sailors and poor people. He used this store to **smuggle** copies of his book into the South. He sewed copies of the book into clothes. People wore the clothes until they got to the South. Then, they gave the hidden books to slaves.

Many people were afraid of David's strong words. Some states passed new laws saying that slaves could not learn to read. The laws were made so that slaves could not read David's book. One group of people in the South offered a reward of $10,000. They said that they would give the money to anyone who caught David. David's friends were scared for him. They begged him to go to Canada. He would be safe there since slavery was against the law. David said no. He said that he would be willing to die to make slaves free.

Not long after that, David Walker was found dead in his home. He might have died of a disease called tuberculosis. The disease affects a person's lungs. His work for slaves ended in one way. But, his powerful words live on.

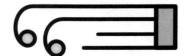
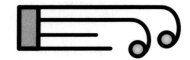

DAVID WALKER
(1785?–1830)

1. The first paragraph is about:

    A. David Walker's book.

    B. David Walker's death.

    C. David Walker's childhood.

    D. David Walker's store.

2. What does the word **smuggle** mean in the story?

    A. sneak in

    B. cuddle

    C. lose

    D. kick

3. Number the following events in the order they happened.

    ____ David Walker writes his book.

    ____ David Walker moves to Boston.

    ____ David Walker is found dead in his home.

    ____ David Walker lives in North Carolina.

    ____ David Walker starts to work for a newspaper.

4. Answer the following questions.

    • Who asked David Walker to move to Canada?

    _____

    • What is the name of David Walker's book?

    _____

    • When did David Walker write his first story about slavery?

    _____

    • How did David Walker get his book to slaves in the South?

    _____

    _____

5. Why would David Walker have been safe in Canada?

    A. Canada did not have slaves or slavery.

    B. Canada was too far away for people to catch him.

    C. Canada was a better place for writers to live.

    D. Canada was a better place for him to hide.

BONUS: Write a story about someone who is trying to get David Walker's book to slaves in the South. What dangers would this person face? Why does this person think the job is an important one?

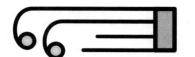
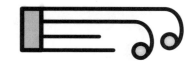

SOJOURNER TRUTH
(1797–1883)

Isabella was a slave who lived in a small Dutch village in New York, sharing a crowded house with her parents and 12 brothers and sisters. She only spoke Dutch. This little girl had a big future waiting for her. She became Sojourner Truth, a famous speaker.

Her life was hard. She was sold several times. One of her masters forced her to marry a man named Thomas. They had five children together. Her master promised to free her. When he didn't, Isabella took her youngest child and ran away.

In 1827, New York State freed all of its slaves. Isabella's son Peter was taken from the state. He had been freed, but he was sold as a slave in the South. Isabella went to court and fought to get him back. She won and brought her son back home again.

It wasn't until 1843 that Isabella decided she would spend her life helping other people. She changed her name to Sojourner Truth. She told a woman named Olive Gilbert about being a slave in the North, and Gilbert wrote a book about Truth's life. Then, she started to give speeches. Sojourner was a powerful speaker. She spoke against slavery, and she spoke for the rights of women. In one speech, she asked her audience, "Ain't I a woman?" And yet, she went on to explain, she had worked as hard as any man she had known. She told her audience that all women are strong and **capable**.

During the Civil War, Sojourner worked to raise money for food and clothing for African American soldiers. She met President Lincoln, who thanked her for her work. After the war ended, Sojourner worked just as hard, raising money for the freed slaves in the South and giving more speeches. She kept working to help people until the day of her death in 1883.

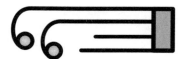

SOJOURNER TRUTH
(1797–1883)

Isabella was a slave who lived in a small Dutch village in New York. She shared a crowded house with her parents and 12 brothers and sisters. She only spoke Dutch. But, this little girl had a big future waiting for her. She grew up to become Sojourner Truth, a famous speaker.

Her life was hard. She was sold several times. One of her masters made her marry a man named Thomas. They had five children. Her master said that he would free her. He didn't, so Isabella ran away with her youngest child.

New York State freed its slaves in 1827. Isabella's son Peter was taken from the state. He had been freed, but he was sold as a slave in the South. Isabella went to court. She fought to get her son back, and she won. Then, she brought her son home again.

In 1843, Isabella decided on a big change. She chose to spend her life helping other people. She changed her name to Sojourner Truth. She told a woman named Olive Gilbert about being a slave in the North. Gilbert wrote a book about Truth's life. Then, Sojourner started to give speeches. She was a great speaker. She spoke against slavery and spoke for the rights of women. In one speech, she asked, "Ain't I a woman?" Then, she explained that she had worked as hard as any man she knew. She said that all women are strong and **capable**.

The Civil War started. Sojourner Truth raised money for black soldiers. She met President Lincoln. He thanked her for her work. After the war ended, Sojourner worked just as hard. She raised money for the freed slaves. She gave more speeches. She worked to help people until the day of her death in 1883.

 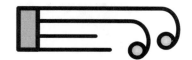

SOJOURNER TRUTH
(1797–1883)

1. The third paragraph is mainly about:

   A. Isabella changing her name.

   B. Isabella's childhood.

   C. Isabella winning a court case to free her son.

   D. Isabella's work during the Civil War.

2. What does the word **capable** mean in the story?

   A. able

   B. quick

   C. weak

   D. soft

3. Number the following events in the order they happened.

   ____ Sojourner Truth works to help the freed slaves.

   ____ Isabella runs away with one of her children.

   ____ Sojourner meets President Lincoln.

   ____ Sojourner starts making speeches.

   ____ Isabella changes her name.

4. Answer the following questions.

   • Who was Thomas?

   _____

   _____

   • What was Sojourner Truth's book about?

   _____

   _____

   • When did Isabella decide to spend her life helping other people?

   _____

   • Where did Isabella live when she was a child?

   _____

5. Why did Sojourner Truth give speeches?

   A. She liked being the center of attention.

   B. She wanted people to know about her family and her life in the Dutch village.

   C. She wanted to tell people slavery was wrong and women are strong.

   D. She wanted to tell people about the time she visited Abraham Lincoln.

BONUS: Imagine that you are Sojourner Truth. Write the first paragraph of a speech you want to make. How will you get people to listen to you? How will you change their minds?

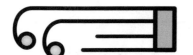

MARIA STEWART
(1803–1879)

Maria Stewart had a big idea. She wanted people to understand that black people and white people are equal. At the time she lived, many people refused to believe that. How could that be changed? Maria thought she had the answer.

Maria Stewart always had strong ideas. She was an **orphan**; her parents died when she was five years old. She took care of herself, working as a servant. Maria was lucky enough to go to school. Later, she married a man who owned his own business preparing ships to go to sea. Maria and her husband lived in Boston, Massachusetts.

But then, her husband died. Some white men stole her husband's money and business after he died, leaving Maria with nothing. The next year, David Walker, a famous African American who wrote and spoke against slavery, died. He was Maria's friend and teacher. These losses were difficult for her.

Maria could have given up hope, but she did not. Instead, she started to write and speak, believing that her losses showed that other people must stand up for their rights. Many people did not like her ideas.

She told African Americans to believe in themselves, find their talents, and put them to use. She told them to be strong and work hard. Above all, she told them to learn everything they could. Nothing, said Maria Stewart, was more important than education.

Maria also thought that women could use her ideas to show that they were as good as men. She suggested that women start their own shops and businesses. She told them to read and think for themselves so that men would see that women were equal to them.

After a time, she stopped giving speeches, but she worked to help people in other ways. She became a teacher. Later, she ran a hospital. All of her life, Maria spoke her mind and worked hard to see that all people were treated fairly.

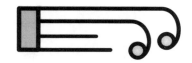

MARIA STEWART
(1803–1879)

Maria Stewart had a big idea. She wanted people to know that black people and white people are equal. At the time she lived, many people did not believe that. How could that be fixed? Maria thought she had the answer.

Maria Stewart always had strong ideas. She was an **orphan**. Her parents died when she was five years old. She had to take care of herself, so she worked as a maid. Maria also went to school. Later, she married. Her husband owned his own business. He got ships ready to go to sea. Maria and her husband lived in Boston, Massachusetts.

But then, her husband died. Some white men stole her husband's money, and Maria was left with nothing. The next year, David Walker died. He was a famous African American who spoke against slavery. He was Maria's friend and teacher. These losses were hard for her.

Maria could have given up hope. But, she did not. She started to write and speak, saying that her losses showed that people must stand up for their rights. Many people did not like her ideas.

She told black people to believe in themselves. She told them to find their talents, be strong, and work hard. She told them to learn everything they could. Nothing was more important than learning.

Maria also thought that women could use her ideas to show that they were as good as men. So, she told women to start their own shops and businesses. She told them to read. She told them to think for themselves. Then, men would understand that they were equal.

Later, she stopped giving speeches. But, she worked to help people in other ways. She became a teacher. Then, she ran a hospital. All of her life, Maria spoke her mind. She worked hard to see that all people were treated fairly.

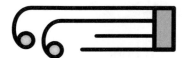

MARIA STEWART
(1803–1879)

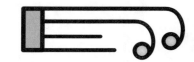

1. Choose a good title for this story.

   A. The Ship Business in the 1800s

   B. A Strong Idea, A Strong Woman

   C. The Schoolteacher

   D. Finding a Way

2. What does the word **orphan** mean in the story?

   A. a person who cannot read

   B. a person who is lost

   C. a person whose parents have died

   D. a person who has a big family

3. Number the following events in the order they happened.

   _____ Maria Stewart becomes a teacher.

   _____ Maria Stewart starts writing and making speeches.

   _____ Maria's parents die.

   _____ The money and business Maria's husband left her are stolen.

   _____ Maria Stewart runs a hospital.

4. Answer the following questions.

   • Who was Maria's friend and teacher?

   _____

   • Where did Maria and her husband live?

   _____

   • What did Maria write and speak about?

   _____

   _____

   • What bad things happened to Maria after her husband died?

   _____

   _____

5. Why do you think that Maria felt so strongly that people had to stand up for their rights?

   A. When her husband's business was stolen from her, she saw that black people were treated differently.

   B. She had not been able to go to school when she was young.

   C. She believed that men were better than women.

   D. She wanted people to help her and make her life easier.

BONUS: List five things that show that all people are equal. Then, write a complete sentence to describe each one.

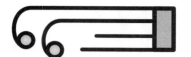
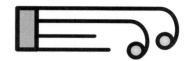

SOLOMON NORTHUP
(1808–18??)

The man named Platt worked in the fields with the other exhausted slaves. Sometimes, when the moon was full, the slaves had to work late into the night. Platt did other chores on the plantation, as well. He fixed broken chairs and the farm wagons. He even knew how to play the fiddle.

Platt had a big secret: he was not really a slave at all. He had been **kidnapped** and sold as a slave. He was really a farmer named Solomon Northup. Solomon was born into a free family and lived in New York with his wife and children. One day

in 1841, he went on a trip, but when he arrived at a hotel in Washington, D.C., he became ill. Two men came into his room and said that they would help him. But instead, they drugged Solomon. When he woke up, he was in chains. Even his name was stolen from him.

The slave seller told Solomon never to say that he was free or he would be killed. Solomon was sold. Then, he was sold again. He was sent to a plantation in Louisiana where he worked for 12 years. Solomon could not send a letter to his family. He had no way to tell them where he was. Gradually, he gave up hope of ever seeing them again.

One day, a white man named Bass came to the plantation. He was a carpenter. Solomon asked Bass where he was from. Bass said that he was from Canada, and Solomon told him that he had been to Canada and to many towns in New York. Then, he told the astonished Bass that he was really a free man. Bass promised to keep Solomon's secret. Together, they wrote a letter asking for help. Then, Bass mailed the letter to New York.

Months went by. Finally, a friend of Solomon's came to the plantation. He had papers from the court that proved that Solomon was free and that he was free to travel back to New York. The plantation owner was angry, but he could not stop Solomon from leaving. Solomon went home to his wife and children. After 12 long years, he was free at last.

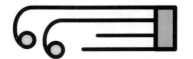

SOLOMON NORTHUP
(1808–18??)

The man named Platt worked in the fields with the other weary slaves. Sometimes, the moon was full. On those nights, the slaves had to work late into the night. Platt did other chores on the plantation, too. He fixed broken chairs. He fixed the farm wagons. He even knew how to play the fiddle.

Platt had a big secret. He was not really a slave at all. He had been **kidnapped**. Then, he had been sold as a slave. He was really a farmer named Solomon Northup. Solomon

was born into a free family. He lived in New York with his wife and children. One day in 1841, he went on a trip. When he got to his hotel in Washington, D.C., he became ill. Two men came into his room. They said that they would help him. But instead, they drugged Solomon. When he woke up, he was in chains. Even his name was stolen from him.

The slave seller told Solomon never to say that he was free. If he did, he would be killed. Solomon was sold. Then, he was sold again. He was sent to a plantation in Louisiana. He worked there for 12 years. Solomon could not send a letter to his family. He had no way to tell them where he was. He gave up hope of ever seeing them again.

One day, a white man named Bass came to the plantation. He was a carpenter. Solomon asked Bass where he was from. Bass said that he was from Canada. Solomon told him that he had been to Canada and to many towns in New York. Bass was very surprised. Then, he told Bass that he was really a free man. Bass promised to keep Solomon's secret. Together, they wrote a letter asking for help. Then, Bass mailed the letter to New York.

Months went by. Finally, a friend of Solomon's came to the plantation. He had papers from the court. The papers said that Solomon was free. They said that he could go home. The plantation owner was angry. But, he could not stop Solomon from leaving. Solomon went home to his wife and children. It had been 12 long years. Now, he was free at last.

 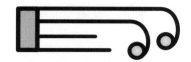

SOLOMON NORTHUP
(1808–18??)

1. What is the main idea of this story?

   A. Solomon Northup was a free man who was sold into slavery and then freed again.

   B. Solomon Northup could fix farm wagons and broken furniture.

   C. Solomon Northup was freed with the help of a man named Bass.

   D. Solomon Northup was sold as a slave, then sold again to a plantation.

2. What does the word **kidnapped** mean in the story?

   A. when someone has borrowed something

   B. a short sleep in the afternoon

   C. caught while stealing something

   D. catching and stealing a human being

3. Number the following events in the order they happened.

   _____ Two men say that they will help Solomon, but instead they drug him.

   _____ Solomon's friend comes with papers from the court to free Solomon.

   _____ A man named Bass helps Solomon send a letter to his family.

   _____ Solomon goes to Washington, D.C.

   _____ Solomon is sold as a slave.

4. Answer the following questions.

   • Where did Solomon Northup live with his wife and children?

   _____

   • What name did Solomon have when he was a slave?

   _____

   • When was Solomon sold as a slave?

   _____

   _____

   • Who was Bass?

   _____

   _____

5. Why do you think Solomon could not let his family know where he was?

   A. He did not have their address, so he could not write to them.

   B. He was a slave, so he was never allowed to mail letters or leave the plantation.

   C. He did not know how to mail a letter.

   D. He was not allowed to use the telephone.

BONUS: Pretend you are one of Solomon Northup's children. His letter asking for help comes to your home. Write a paragraph about how you feel after so many years of not knowing where your father was.

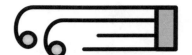

FREDERICK DOUGLASS
(1818–1895)

The kind mistress was teaching a slave child to read when her husband came into the room. He shouted at his wife and told her it was against the law to teach a slave to read. He said that any slave who knew how to read would not **obey** his master. The slave listened carefully. He now understood that reading was a door to freedom. The child's name was Frederick Bailey.

Frederick was born in Maryland. He was a slave until he was a young man. He worked in the fields. Then, he was sent to Baltimore to work on ships. His master even let him keep some of the money he made. He did not know that Frederick was planning to use the money to run away.

One day in 1838, Frederick put on a sailor's uniform. He had forged papers that said he was free. He took a train to Philadelphia, Pennsylvania, and another to New York. A man there who worked on the Underground Railroad helped Frederick get to Massachusetts. Frederick changed his last name to Douglass because this would make it harder for his master to find him.

Frederick Douglass started to write about his life as a slave. He published a book and gave speeches. Later, he started his own newspaper called the *North Star*. His newspaper became famous. It published stories about the mistreatment of slaves and pieces about the wrongs of slavery.

The Civil War started. Frederick Douglass wanted President Lincoln to let black people fight in the war. He wanted the President to free the slaves. He met with President Lincoln. Douglass was the first African American to be asked to visit the White House as a guest. Lincoln listened carefully to Douglass's opinions, and the two men became friends.

After the war, Frederick Douglass kept working and fighting for the rights of freed slaves. He kept giving speeches. Many people said that he was the greatest speaker of his day. He was a strong supporter of freedom and equality.

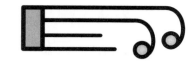

FREDERICK DOUGLASS
(1818–1895)

The kind mistress was teaching a slave child to read. Then, her husband came into the room. He shouted at his wife. He told her that it was against the law to teach a slave to read. He said that a slave who knew how to read would not **obey** his master. The slave listened carefully. He now knew that reading was a door to freedom. The child's name was Frederick Bailey.

Frederick was born in Maryland. He was a slave until he was a young man. He worked in the fields. Then, he worked on ships. His master let him keep some of the money he made. He did not know that Frederick was planning to run away.

One day in 1838, Frederick dressed as a sailor. He had fake papers that said he was free. He took a train to Philadelphia, Pennsylvania. Then, he went to New York. A man there helped Frederick get to Massachusetts. Frederick changed his last name. He chose the name Douglass. This made it harder for his master to find him.

Frederick Douglass wrote about his life as a slave. He wrote a book and gave speeches. He started a newspaper. It was called the *North Star*. Many people read his newspaper. It had stories that showed that slavery was wrong.

The Civil War started. Frederick Douglass wanted President Lincoln to let black people fight in the war. He wanted the President to free the slaves. He met with President Lincoln. Douglass was asked to visit the White House. He was the first African American to be asked there as a guest. Lincoln listened carefully to what Douglass said. The two men became friends.

After the war, Frederick Douglass kept working. He fought for the rights of freed slaves. He kept giving speeches. Many people said that he was the greatest speaker of his day. He was a strong voice for freedom and equal rights.

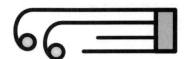

FREDERICK DOUGLASS
(1818–1895)

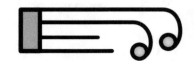

1. What is the main idea of the third paragraph?

   A. Frederick Douglass learned to read.

   B. Frederick Douglass started a newspaper.

   C. Frederick Douglass escaped from slavery.

   D. Frederick Douglass met with President Lincoln.

2. What does the word **obey** mean in the story?

   A. act against

   B. run swiftly

   C. be quiet

   D. follow orders

3. Number the following events in the order they happened.

   ____ Frederick goes to work on ships.

   ____ Frederick starts a newspaper.

   ____ Frederick changes his last name to Douglass.

   ____ Frederick goes to the White House to meet with Lincoln.

   ____ Frederick is born in Maryland.

4. Answer the following questions.

   • What was the *North Star*?

   _____

   _____

   • How did Frederick travel to the North?

   _____

   _____

   • In what year did Frederick run away?

   _____

   • With whom did Frederick Douglass meet during the Civil War?

   _____

5. Why do you think Frederick Douglass wrote a book?

   A. He wanted to tell stories that people would enjoy.

   B. He wanted people to know what it was like to be a slave.

   C. He wanted to be famous.

   D. He wanted to advertise his newspaper.

BONUS: Frederick Douglass felt that reading was an important way to become free. Write a paragraph about how you feel about reading.

HARRIET TUBMAN
(1819?–1913)

The slave woman looked up in the sky at the North Star. She found her way carefully from one friendly house to another. In this way, Harriet Tubman escaped using the Underground Railroad. This was a secret **system** of safe houses and helpful people. They helped slaves get to freedom. Harriet ran away to Philadelphia, Pennsylvania. She knew she could live there as a free person.

Running away from slavery was difficult and dangerous. If slaves were caught, they would be sent back to slavery. But, Harriet was very brave. Once she was free, she wanted to help other slaves become free, too. She could

have stayed where she was safe in her new home in Philadelphia. Instead, she returned to the South.

First, she helped her sister and her sister's children escape from slavery. Then, she went back to help other slaves.

Harriet worked this way for 10 years, from 1850 to 1860. She may have guided as many as 300 slaves to the North and freedom. Then, the Civil War started. Harriet was not going to stop helping people. She chose to do something that was even more dangerous than her Underground Railroad work.

Harriet became a spy. She had helped slaves travel across the land in the South. So, she knew ways to travel secretly without being caught. She spied on soldiers at their camps. She learned information that helped the army in the North. Harriet even led a group of black soldiers on a raid during which the group freed over 700 slaves. No other woman had ever led American soldiers on a raid. Nothing could stop Harriet from helping people who needed her.

When she was not spying, Harriet worked as a nurse. She helped care for African American soldiers and slaves who were wounded. After the war, Harriet helped freed slaves. She worked for the rights of women. She also opened a home to take care of old people. Harriet Tubman was one of the strongest and bravest women in American history.

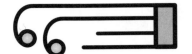
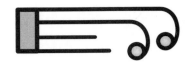

HARRIET TUBMAN
(1819?–1913)

The slave woman looked up in the sky at the North Star. She found her way from one friendly house to another. Harriet Tubman was running away. She used the Underground Railroad for help. This was a secret **system** of safe houses and people. They helped slaves get to freedom. Harriet went to Philadelphia, Pennsylvania. She knew she could live there as a free person.

Running away from slavery was hard. It was filled with danger. If slaves were caught, they would be sent back to slavery. But, Harriet was very brave. Once she was free, she wanted to help other slaves become free, too. She could have stayed where she was safe. Instead, she went back to the South.

First, she helped her sister and her sister's children run away. Then, she went back to help other slaves.

Harriet worked this way for 10 years. She may have helped as many as 300 slaves run away from 1850 to 1860. Then, the Civil War started. Harriet was not going to stop helping people. She chose new work. It was filled with even more danger.

Harriet became a spy. She had helped slaves travel across the land in the South. So, she knew ways to travel without being caught. She watched soldiers. She found out things to help the army in the North. Harriet even led a group of black soldiers on a raid. During the raid, the group freed over 700 slaves. No other woman had ever led American soldiers on a raid. Nothing could stop Harriet. She wanted to help people who needed her.

When she was not spying, Harriet worked as a nurse. She cared for black soldiers and slaves who were hurt. After the war, Harriet helped freed slaves. She worked for the rights of women. She opened a home to take care of old people. She was one of the strongest and bravest women in American history.

HARRIET TUBMAN
(1819?–1913)

1. Choose a good title for this story.

   A. The Spy

   B. The Underground Railroad

   C. The Escaped Slave

   D. Working for Freedom

2. What does the word **system** mean in the story?

   A. a planned arrangement

   B. something secret

   C. a mess

   D. a type of money

3. Number the following events in the order they happened.

   ____ Harriet Tubman opens a home to care for old people.

   ____ Harriet uses the Underground Railroad to get to Philadelphia.

   ____ Harriet Tubman lives as a slave in the South.

   ____ Harriet Tubman leads a raid during the Civil War.

   ____ Harriet Tubman helps hundreds of slaves travel to freedom.

4. Answer the following questions.

   • What was the Underground Railroad?

   _____

   _____

   • When did Harriet Tubman work on the Underground Railroad?

   _____

   • Who were the first slaves Harriet went South to help?

   _____

   • How did Harriet Tubman help the North during the Civil War?

   _____

   _____

5. Why did Harriet leave safety in the North to go back to the South?

   A. She liked the South better.

   B. She wanted to help free family members and other slaves.

   C. She was afraid she would be caught.

   D. She wanted to help the army in the South.

BONUS: Write about another brave woman that you know or have read about.

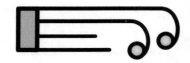

ROBERT SMALLS
(1839–1915)

It was 1862. Charleston, South Carolina, the place where the Civil War started, was a stronghold of the South. The town's harbor was long and deep and dotted with forts, including Fort Sumter. Beyond the fort were the Union gunboats, blocking the harbor. It was a dangerous place to be.

Nobody knew that better than Robert Smalls. A slave who worked on the boats and docks, Smalls knew every inch of the harbor. He knew the secret signal that pilots used to get past the forts. He knew all of this because he had to steer ships across the harbor himself, delivering supplies to the forts. In May, 1862, Smalls chose to use this knowledge for a different purpose.

He and some other slaves thought of a bold plan. They would take the steamship they worked on, the *Planter*, out at night. They would steer it past each of the forts, as if they were going to deliver **supplies** to the next one. Then, they would race past Fort Sumter to the Union gunboats. They would hand over the *Planter*—carrying guns, cannons, and ammunition—to the North. By doing this, they would win their freedom.

On the night of May 12, Smalls and his friends were on board. Smalls put on the coat and hat of the *Planter*'s captain. He could imitate the way the captain stood and walked. The ship left the dock and stopped to secretly pick up the families of the men on board. Then, it set off on its dangerous way.

Each fort hailed the ship. Smalls answered with the right signal. By the time the ship reached Fort Sumter, the sun was rising. Would the guards see that Smalls was black? He folded his arms and lowered his head, letting the big straw hat shade his face. The guard let the ship pass! Then, the *Planter* raced toward the Union gunboats in the open water. Would the Northern boats fire at the *Planter*? Smalls had planned for this, too. He took down the Southern flag and put up a white bedsheet in its place. A Northern captain saw the white flag and came on board. Smalls presented him with the *Planter*, her cargo, and secrets about the Charleston harbor. Smalls was a Union hero! Even better, he was a free man.

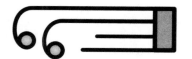 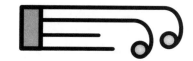

ROBERT SMALLS
(1839–1915)

It was 1862. Charleston, South Carolina, was the place where the Civil War started. Now, it was guarded. The town's harbor was long and deep and dotted with forts, including Fort Sumter. Past the fort were gunboats from the North. They blocked the harbor. It was a dangerous place to be.

Nobody knew that better than Robert Smalls. Smalls was a slave. He worked on the ships and docks. Smalls knew every inch of the harbor. He knew the secret signal to get past the forts. He knew all of this because he had to steer ships through the harbor, taking **supplies** to the forts. But one night in May, 1862, Smalls used this knowledge for a different job.

Smalls and some other slaves had a bold plan. The steamship they worked on was called the *Planter*. They would take the ship out at night. They would go past each one of the forts. They would make it look like they were going to the next fort in line. Then, they would race past the last fort, Fort Sumter. They would go to the ships that belonged to the North. They would hand over the *Planter* and all of the guns and cargo on board. By doing this, they would win their freedom.

On the night of May 12, Smalls and his friends were on the ship. Smalls put on the captain's coat and hat. He could stand and walk like the captain. The ship left the dock. It stopped to secretly pick up the men's families. Then, the ship set off on its dangerous way.

Each fort called to the ship. Smalls sent the right signal back. By the time the ship reached Fort Sumter, the sun was up. Would the guards see that Smalls was a black man? He folded his arms. He tipped his head down. The big straw hat shaded his face. The guard let the ship pass! Then, the *Planter* raced toward the Northern gunboats. Would the Northern boats fire at the *Planter*? Smalls had planned for this, too. He took down the Southern flag. He put up a white bedsheet. A Northern captain saw the white flag. He came on board. Smalls gave him the *Planter* and the ship's cargo. He told the captain secrets about the Charleston harbor. Smalls was a Union hero! Even better, he was a free man.

ROBERT SMALLS
(1839–1915)

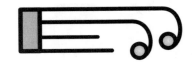

1. Choose a good title for this story.

   A. A Dangerous Escape

   B. Charleston in the Civil War

   C. Fort Sumter

   D. Pilots in the Civil War

2. What does the word **supplies** mean in the story?

   A. free gifts

   B. the wheel used to steer a ship

   C. food, clothing, and other things that people need

   D. something that is easy to put into different shapes

3. Number the following events in the order they happened.

   _____ Smalls and his friends make a plan to escape.

   _____ The ship stops to pick up the families of the men on board.

   _____ Smalls puts on the captain's hat and coat.

   _____ Smalls gives the right signal to each fort.

   _____ Smalls gives the ship to a Northern captain.

4. Answer the following questions.

   • Who was Robert Smalls?

   _____

   _____

   • What was the name of the ship that Robert Smalls took?

   _____

   • Where did Robert Smalls live?

   _____

   • How did Smalls signal to the Northern ship that he was a friend?

   _____

   _____

5. Why was Robert Smalls a good person to carry out his plan?

   A. He wanted to be free.

   B. He knew how to get around the harbor and past the forts.

   C. He really wanted to help the South win the war.

   D. He could not steer the ship.

BONUS: Pretend that you were one of the children on board the ship when Robert Smalls took it out of the harbor. What was the trip like? Write a paragraph telling about the trip and your feelings.

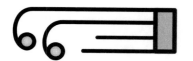
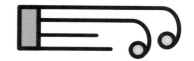

DANIEL HALE WILLIAMS
(1856?–1931)

In the 1800s, people did not understand much about germs. That made it hard to **operate** on people who needed a doctor's help. Doctors did not like to cut into a living person's chest to fix the heart. If they were forced to do this, the patient usually died from infection.

That's why Daniel Hale Williams's work was so important. He was the first doctor to do an open-heart operation on a human without the patient dying. Daniel helped a man named James Cornish who had been stabbed. He fixed a problem with James's heart. Then, he sewed him closed again. This was in 1893. James Cornish lived another 20 years after Dr. Williams operated on him!

Daniel came from a happy family. But, his father died when Daniel was young. Mrs. Williams could not handle raising her children alone. She decided they would live with family members. Everyone was sad when the family was separated. Daniel was supposed to learn to be a cobbler, but he did not want to make shoes.

At first, Daniel worked as a barber like his father. Then, he went to work for a doctor, and that's when Daniel decided he wanted to be a doctor, too. He attended medical school in Chicago, Illinois, and graduated in 1883. Then, he took care of African American patients. At that time, there were only three other African American doctors in Chicago.

Later, he started the first hospital in the United States that treated both black people and white people. He also started a nursing school for African Americans. After he saved James Cornish's life, Daniel became famous. He gave talks about medicine. In 1913, he became the first African American member of the American College of Surgeons. His life was dedicated to giving medical care and help to people of all races.

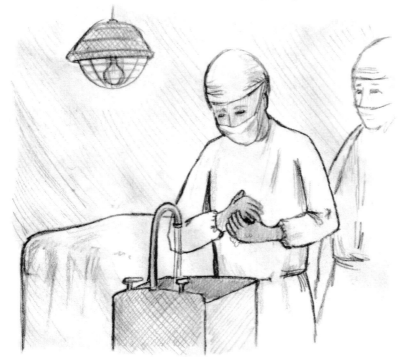

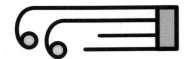

DANIEL HALE WILLIAMS
(1856?–1931)

In the 1800s, people did not know much about germs. That made it hard to **operate** on people who needed a doctor's help. Doctors did not like to cut into a person's chest. If they had to try, the person often died from infection.

That's why Daniel Hale Williams's work was so important. He was the first doctor to operate on a heart without the patient dying. Daniel helped a man named James Cornish. James had been stabbed. Dr. Williams fixed his heart. Then, he sewed James closed again. This was in 1893. James Cornish lived for another 20 years after Daniel helped him!

Daniel came from a happy family. But, his father died when Daniel was young. Mrs. Williams could not care for her children alone. She sent them to live with family members. Everyone was sad when the family was separated. Daniel was supposed to learn to make shoes, but he did not want to.

At first, Daniel worked as a barber. This is what his father did. Then, he went to work for a doctor. That's when Daniel knew he wanted to be a doctor, too. He went to school in Chicago, Illinois, to learn to be a doctor. He became a doctor in 1883. Then, he took care of black patients. Daniel was one of only four African American doctors in Chicago at that time.

Later, Daniel started the first hospital in the United States for both black people and white people. He also started a school for black nurses. Daniel became well-known for saving James Cornish's life. He gave talks about his work. He became the first African American member of the American College of Surgeons in 1913. He spent his life giving care and help to people of all races.

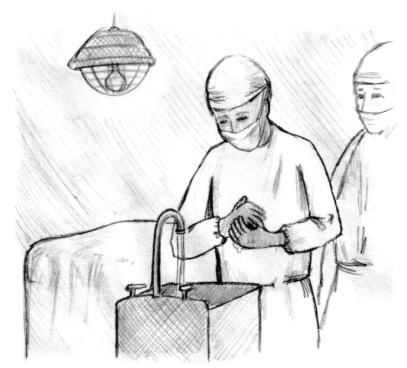

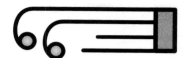

DANIEL HALE WILLIAMS
(1856?–1931)

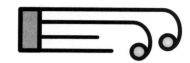

1. The third paragraph is mainly about:

   A. Daniel Hale Williams's childhood.

   B. the different jobs Daniel had.

   C. the famous work Daniel did.

   D. the hospitals Daniel started.

2. What does the word **operate** mean in the story?

   A. multiply

   B. send away

   C. to perform surgery

   D. number

3. Number the following events in the order they happened.

   ____ Daniel's mother sent her children to live with family members.

   ____ Daniel saves the life of a patient with a heart operation.

   ____ Daniel goes to work for a doctor.

   ____ Daniel starts a nursing school.

   ____ Daniel works as a barber.

4. Answer the following questions.

   • Who was James Cornish?

   _____

   _____

   • What job did Daniel not want to do?

   _____

   • Where did Daniel go to school to be a doctor?

   _____

   • How did Daniel become famous?

   _____

   _____

5. Why do you think Daniel started a nursing school?

   A. There were no other schools for nurses.

   B. Nurses did not get a good education.

   C. He wanted to help black people who wanted to be nurses.

   D. He wanted the money from the school.

BONUS: Do you know what you want to be when you grow up? Write about your plans.

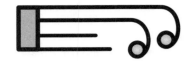

BOOKER T. WASHINGTON
(1856–1915)

Booker T. Washington was born a slave. After slaves were freed, he worked in a mine. One day, he heard two miners discussing a school for black people. Booker found a way to attend the school. He worked hard. He later wrote that he could never remember playing—not even as a small child.

When he finished school, Booker wanted to help other black people learn, so he started the Tuskegee Institute in Alabama in 1881. At the beginning, the school was just a small shack. Booker wanted to use the school to train teachers. Then, he added more classes to help African Americans learn new jobs. At the school, students actually helped build the buildings. They planted and grew their own food. They went to classes. Students got up at 5:00 in the morning, and classes lasted until 9:30 at night!

Booker believed that hard work was important. He worked hard, too. He found people to donate money to the school. He bought 540 acres of land. By 1888, over 400 students were attending his school. Students worked alongside Booker to keep building the school.

Some black people did not agree with what Booker was doing. They worried that he was too friendly with white people and their ideas. They said that he thought like a white person. Booker gave a speech in which he said that black people and white people could work together but should stay apart otherwise. He said that black people and white people were like different fingers on the same hand. Other African Americans wanted to fight so that black people and white people had the same schools and neighborhoods, but Booker did not think that was important.

When Booker died, over 8,000 people came to his funeral at the school he **founded** to say good-bye to a great teacher.

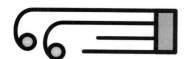

BOOKER T. WASHINGTON
(1856–1915)

Booker T. Washington was born a slave. After slaves were freed, he worked in a mine. One day, he heard two miners talking about a school for black people. Booker found a way to go to the school. He worked hard. He later wrote that he never played—not even when he was a small child.

When he finished school, Booker wanted to help other black people learn. He started a school in 1881. It was called the Tuskegee Institute. At first, the school was just a small shack. Booker wanted to use the school to train teachers. Then, he added more classes. These helped black people learn new jobs. At the school, students helped build the buildings. They planted and grew their own food. They went to classes. Students got up at 5:00 in the morning. Classes lasted until 9:30 at night!

Booker thought hard work was important. He worked hard, too. He found people to give money to the school. He bought land. By 1888, over 400 students went to his school. Students worked with Booker to keep building the school.

Some black people did not like what Booker was doing. They thought he was too friendly with white people. They said that Booker thought like a white person. Booker gave a speech where he said that black people and white people could work together. But, he said, they should stay apart when they were not working. He said that black people and white people were like different fingers on the same hand. Others wanted black people and white people to have the same schools and neighborhoods. Booker did not think that was important.

When he died, over 8,000 people came to his funeral. It was held at the school he had **founded**. They said good-bye to a great teacher.

BOOKER T. WASHINGTON
(1856–1915)

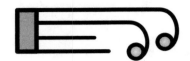

1. The second paragraph is mainly about:

   A. the school Booker started.

   B. Booker's childhood.

   C. Booker's ideas about black people and white people.

   D. Booker's work in a mine.

2. What does the word **founded** mean in the story?

   A. made of iron

   B. not lost

   C. started

   D. corrected

3. Number the following events in the order they happened.

   _____ Eight thousand people come to Booker's funeral.

   _____ Booker is freed from slavery.

   _____ Booker starts a school in a small shack.

   _____ Booker gives a speech saying that white people and black people should work together but live apart.

   _____ Booker buys land for his school and has students help him build it.

4. Answer the following questions.

   • What was the Tuskegee Institute?

   _____

   _____

   • Who went to the Tuskegee Institute?

   _____

   • Where did Booker hear about a school for black people?

   _____

   • How long was a school day at the Tuskegee Institute?

   _____

   _____

5. Why do you think some black people did not like Booker's ideas?

   A. They wanted everything to be equal for black people and white people.

   B. They wanted white people's jobs.

   C. Booker believed in hard work.

   D. Booker did not speak well.

BONUS: What do you think is the most important thing about going to school? Write a paragraph to explain your opinion.

GEORGE WASHINGTON CARVER
(1861?–1943)

George Washington Carver loved plants. When he was young, he lived on a farm. When he grew up, he chose to educate other people about plants, but he was also a great **inventor**. He found new ways to use plants that other people had ignored. These ideas made him famous and also helped people around the world.

George taught at the Tuskegee Institute, founded by Booker T. Washington. He was paid very little there, but he wanted to help other African Americans learn.

George believed that farmers in the South needed help. Many of them planted cotton. This plant can exhaust the soil. When that happens, crops fail. George wanted people to plant different crops in different years to help restore the soil. He thought peanuts and sweet potatoes would be good crops for this plan. But first, he needed other people to understand the value of these plants.

So, George started inventing new ways to use these plants. He thought of hundreds of ideas. He showed people how to make ink and glue from sweet potatoes. He showed them how to make soap, dye, shampoo, and paper from peanuts. He was also the first person to make peanut butter! George did not sell his ideas or try to patent them. He gave his ideas away for free so that farmers could use them.

People loved George's ideas. The great inventor Thomas Edison asked George to come to work with him. George said that he would rather stay at Tuskegee and turned down Edison's offer—equal to one million dollars in today's money—just to stay there and teach. When he died, he was buried at the school he loved so much.

George Washington Carver loved plants. When he was young, he lived on a farm. When he grew up, he taught other people about plants. He was also a great **inventor**. He thought of new ideas about plants. These ideas made him famous. His ideas also helped people around the world.

George taught at the school started by Booker T. Washington. He was paid very little there. He worked there to help other black people learn.

George thought farmers in the South needed help. Many of them planted cotton. This plant can make the soil tired. Crops die when the soil is bad. George wanted people to plant different crops in different years. This would help the soil. He thought peanuts and sweet potatoes would be good crops. He needed other people to think these plants had value, too.

So, George thought of new ways to use these plants. He had hundreds of ideas. He showed people how to make ink and glue from sweet potatoes. He showed them how to make soap, dye, shampoo, and paper from peanuts. He was also the first person to make peanut butter! George did not sell his ideas. He gave them away for free. He wanted farmers to be able to use his ideas.

People loved George's ideas. Thomas Edison asked George to come to work with him. George said no. He wanted to keep teaching. He turned down a lot of money—equal to one million dollars in today's money—just to stay and teach. When he died, he was buried at the school he loved so much.

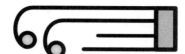 GEORGE WASHINGTON CARVER
(1861?–1943)

1. Choose a good title for this story.

    A. The Man Who Hated Teaching

    B. Slavery in the South

    C. A Genius with Plants

    D. Thomas Edison's Friend

2. What does the word **inventor** mean in the story?

    A. a way of using plants

    B. someone who thinks of new ideas or products

    C. someone who fixes things on farms

    D. a subject at school

3. Number the following events in the order they happened.

    ____ Thomas Edison asks George to work with him.

    ____ George is buried at the school where he taught.

    ____ George finds new ways to use peanuts.

    ____ George starts teaching.

    ____ George grows up on a farm.

4. Answer the following questions.

    • What did George Washington Carver teach farmers about?

    _____

    • Who started the school where George taught?

    _____

    • In what part of the country did George think that farmers needed help?

    _____

    • How did George show people that peanuts and sweet potatoes had value?

    _____

    _____

5. Why do you think George did not sell his ideas?

    A. He wanted as many people to use them as possible.

    B. He did not want poor people to be kept from using his ideas.

    C. He wanted farmers to grow the new crops.

    D. all of the above

BONUS: Think about a plant that you like. It can be a plant for food, a flower, or a houseplant. Write a paragraph telling why you like this plant and how it can be used.

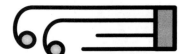
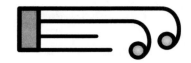

IDA B. WELLS-BARNETT
(1862–1931)

Ida B. Wells-Barnett was a woman who would not be stopped. This brave woman worked for equal rights her entire life.

Ida's parents died when she was 16 years old. Ida decided to take care of her five brothers and sisters by herself. She found a teaching job and made a home for her family.

The laws at the time said that black people could not sit in the same sections of a train as white people. In 1884, Ida took a train trip and sat in the white people's train car. She would not move. Two men dragged her out of the white people's car, so Ida sued the railroad and won.

Ida lived in Memphis, Tennessee. She helped start a newspaper there. She was not afraid to say what she thought, writing stories in the paper about black people who were being attacked and killed. She told black people that they should move to the West, where it would be safer for them.

Then, Ida had to move herself. People were angry about her writing, which put her in danger. A **mob** of angry people went to her office and broke in. They smashed furniture and tore up papers. Ida retreated to England but not to hide. Instead, she gave many speeches about black people and how they were being treated in the United States. Later, she came home to America and kept writing and giving speeches. Nothing could stop her.

Ida moved to Chicago, Illinois, and married a lawyer. They started another newspaper together. Ida also started a club for black women called the Alpha Suffrage Club. The club taught black women about their rights. The women studied government and how it worked, and they also worked to change the laws so that women could vote.

Women's groups from around the country went to Washington, D.C., in 1913. They marched in protest for the right to vote. Each group was supposed to march with other people from the same state. But, Ida's group was told that they could not march with white women from Illinois. Instead, the black women were all told they had to march at the end of the parade. Ida refused. She marched with the Illinois group, walking between two white friends. Many newspapers ran the story about her brave stand. It was a symbolic choice for Ida, who worked for equal rights until she died in 1931. Only death stopped this amazing woman.

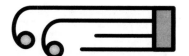 

IDA B. WELLS-BARNETT
(1862–1931)

Ida B. Wells-Barnett was a woman who would not be stopped. This brave woman worked for equal rights her whole life.

Ida's parents died when she was 16 years old. Ida chose to take care of her five brothers and sisters by herself. She found a teaching job. She made a home for her family.

The laws at the time said that black people could not sit in the same cars of a train as white people. In 1884, Ida took a train trip. She sat in the train car for white people. She would not move. Two men dragged her out. Ida sued the railroad. She won.

Ida lived in Memphis, Tennessee. She helped start a newspaper there. She was not afraid to say what she thought. Ida wrote stories in the paper. The stories were about black people who were being attacked and killed. She told black people that they should move to the West. She thought it would be safer for them there.

Then, Ida had to move herself. People were angry about her writing. This put her in danger. A **mob** of angry people went to her office. They broke in. They broke furniture. They tore up papers. Ida went to England. She did not hide. She gave many speeches about black people. She told how they were treated. Then, she came home to America. She kept writing and giving speeches. Nothing could stop her.

Ida moved to Chicago, Illinois. She married a lawyer. They started another newspaper together. Ida also started a club for black women. It was called the Alpha Suffrage Club. The club taught black women about their rights. The women studied government and how it worked. The club also worked to change the laws so that women could vote.

Women's groups from around the country went to Washington, D.C., in 1913. They marched for the right to vote. Each group was going to march with other people from the same state. But Ida's group was told that they could not march with white women from Illinois. Instead, the black women were told to march at the end of the parade. Ida said no. She marched with the Illinois group. She walked with two white friends. Many newspapers ran the story about her brave stand. Ida worked for equal rights until she died in 1931. Only death stopped her.

IDA B. WELLS-BARNETT
(1862–1931)

1. Choose a good title for this story.

   A. The Woman Who Would Not Be Stopped

   B. The Alpha Suffrage Club

   C. A Woman's Right to Vote

   D. Newspaper Women of the 1800s

2. What does the word **mob** mean in the story?

   A. a club for women

   B. a group of angry people

   C. a type of cap

   D. a kind of school

3. Number the following events in the order they happened.

   _____ Ida starts a club for black women.

   _____ Ida gives speeches in England.

   _____ Ida marches for the vote in Washington, D.C.

   _____ Ida becomes a teacher to take care of her brothers and sisters.

   _____ Ida starts a newspaper in Memphis, Tennessee.

4. Answer the following questions.

   • What did the Alpha Suffrage Club do?

   _____

   _____

   • Who did Ida sue in 1884?

   _____

   • Where did Ida go when her newspaper office was destroyed?

   _____

   • How did Ida fight back when she was told to march at the end of the parade?

   _____

   _____

5. Why wouldn't Ida march at the end of the parade?

   A. She thought that black women and white women from each state should march together.

   B. She thought that no one would be able to see her if she was at the end.

   C. She did not want to march for women's right to vote.

   D. none of the above

BONUS: Pretend that you were one of the people watching the parade for women's rights in 1913. Write a letter to the editor of a newspaper about Ida's actions.

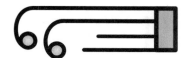

MARY CHURCH TERRELL
(1863–1954)

Mary Church Terrell, called Mollie, was born in Memphis, Tennessee, to parents who were once slaves. After they were freed, her father became a very rich man. Mollie was raised in comfort and luxury. Her father wanted her to be a lady, which in those days meant living quietly and in a refined way. But, Mollie had a different plan for her life.

Mollie went to college in Ohio and became a teacher. Then, she got married. Her husband, Robert Terrell, was a lawyer. Mollie decided that she wanted to help black women. She started giving speeches about the condition of African American women in the United States. She talked about how it had been a short time since slaves were freed. Since then, some black women, like herself, had gone to college. But, other women were still living in one-room cabins, and their lives were almost identical to the lives of slaves. Mollie wanted to change things. She said that in order to change things, black people had to have the same chances as white people.

So, Mollie fought for the right to vote. She also fought against segregation, which kept black people from going to the same schools as white people. African Americans could not sit in the same seats on the trains or buses as white people. Laws like these, often called "separate but equal" laws, kept black people apart and made life difficult for them. Mollie even wrote a book about her life, showing how wrong it was to keep people separated by race.

Mollie found a set of laws that had been passed in the 1870s. These laws said that all people could go to the same **public** places. She researched these laws and discovered they had never been overturned by the courts. That meant keeping black people separate was actually against the law!

Mollie fought to have the laws enforced. She worked for this for the rest of her life. She wrote for newspapers. She gave speeches. In the year that Mollie died, 1954, the courts finally said that separate places for white people and black people were not equal. Mollie had won at last.

 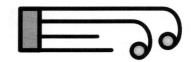

MARY CHURCH TERRELL
(1863–1954)

Mary Church Terrell, called Mollie, was born in Memphis, Tennessee. Her parents had been slaves. Then, they were set free. Her father was a very rich man. Mollie was raised in comfort. Her father wanted her to be a lady. In those days, that meant living quietly. Mollie had a different plan for her life.

Mollie went to college in Ohio. She became a teacher. Then, she got married. Her husband, Robert Terrell, was a lawyer. Mollie wanted to help black women. She started to give speeches. She talked about how it had been a short time since slaves were freed. Some black women, like herself, had gone to college. But, other women were still living in one-room cabins. Their lives were almost the same as the lives of slaves. Mollie wanted to change things. She said that in order to change things, black people had to have the same chances as white people.

So, Mollie fought for the right to vote. She also fought against the way that black people were kept from going to the same schools as white people. They could not sit in the same seats on the trains or buses as white people. These laws were sometimes called "separate but equal" laws. They kept black people apart. It made life harder for them. Mollie even wrote a book about her life. It showed how wrong it was to keep people apart.

Mollie found a set of laws that passed in the 1870s. These laws said that all people could go to the same **public** places. She read about the laws. She found out that these laws had never been changed by the court. That meant keeping black people separated was against the law!

Mollie fought to have the laws enforced. She worked for this for the rest of her life. She wrote for newspapers. She gave speeches. In the year that Mollie died, 1954, the courts finally said that separate places for white people and black people were not equal. Mollie had won at last.

THE
Progress of Colo
Women
BY
MARY CHURCH TERR

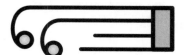

MARY CHURCH TERRELL
(1863–1954)

1. The fifth paragraph is mainly about Mollie's:

   A. childhood.

   B. marriage.

   C. fight for the right to vote.

   D. fight to put laws into effect.

2. What does the word **public** mean in the story?

   A. private and kept separate

   B. widely spread

   C. open to and shared by the community

   D. someone who is in favor of freedom

3. Number the following events in the order they happened.

   ____ Mollie starts giving speeches.

   ____ Mollie goes to college.

   ____ Mollie sees the end of "separate but equal" laws in the last year of her life.

   ____ Mollie's parents are set free.

   ____ Mollie finds an old set of laws that say that public places should be open to everyone.

4. Answer the following questions.

   • What was Mollie's childhood like?

   _____

   _____

   • Who did Mollie marry?

   _____

   • Where was Mollie born?

   _____

   • How did Mollie fight against separation of the races?

   _____

   _____

5. Why did Mollie spend her life fighting to make things equal for African Americans?

   A. She cared about fairness.

   B. She cared about African Americans.

   C. She wanted black people to have the same chances as white people.

   D. all of the above

BONUS: Write a paragraph telling why keeping some people out of schools or public places is not fair.

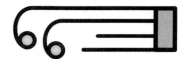 

MATTHEW HENSON
(1866–1955)

The man stood in the cold, white world. He looked around him and waited for the other sleds to arrive. Then, he looked north and suddenly realized he was standing farther north than any other person in history had ever stood.

The explorer was an African American man named Matthew Henson. He was on an expedition with Robert Peary to the north pole, but it was not the first time Matthew Henson had made this journey. He had worked for Peary for over 20 years. He had been with Peary all of the times the explorer had tried to make it to the north pole and failed. They were not alone in their goals and their failures. Hundreds of men had already died trying to get to the north pole.

Each time Peary's team tried to make it to the pole, something happened to turn the explorers back from their destination. One time, they nearly starved to death due to a lack of supplies. Another time, they could not keep going north because of melting ice. Finally, in 1908, Peary decided to try one last time. He insisted that Matthew Henson go with him. "Henson must go all the way," said Peary. "I cannot make it without him."

Matthew Henson learned a great deal in his work with Peary. He knew how to survive in the Arctic. He got along with the natives and learned their language. He used their information to help him make plans for the final expedition. Henson's plans with Peary were precise. The team put **caches**, or stockpiles, of food in igloos along the trail. They would use this food on their way back after they ran out of supplies from the sleds. Henson was the best driver of the dog teams, so he took the lead and broke the trail. This time, at last, the team found success. On April 6, 1909, Matthew Henson stood with Peary and their crew at the northernmost tip of the world.

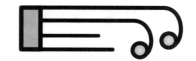

MATTHEW HENSON
(1866–1955)

The man stood in the cold, white world. He looked around him and waited for the other sleds to arrive. Then, he looked north. Suddenly, he knew he was standing farther north than any other person in history had ever stood.

The explorer was an African American man named Matthew Henson. He was exploring with Robert Peary. They were going to the north pole. It was not the first time Matthew Henson had made this trip. He had worked for Peary for over 20 years. He had been with Peary all of the times the explorer had tried to make it to the north pole. They were not the only ones who had this goal. Hundreds of men had already died trying to get to the north pole.

Each time, something happened that made Peary and his team turn back from their goal. One time, they almost starved to death. Another time, they could not keep going north because of melting ice. Finally, in 1908, Peary said that he would try one last time. He insisted that Matthew Henson go with him. "Henson must go all the way," said Peary. "I cannot make it without him."

Matthew Henson learned a lot in his work with Peary. He knew how to live in the Arctic. He got along with the natives. He learned their language. They told Henson things that helped him make plans. On this trip, Henson helped Peary make a careful plan. The team put **caches**, or stockpiles, of food in igloos along the trail. They would use this food on the way back. Henson was the best driver of the dog teams. He took the lead. He broke the trail. This time, at last, the team found success. On April 6, 1909, Matthew Henson stood with Peary and their crew at the northern tip of the world.

MATTHEW HENSON
(1866–1955)

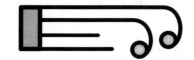

1. Choose a good title for this story.

   A. An African American Goes South

   B. An African American Explores the Arctic

   C. How Peary Reached the north pole

   D. Matthew Henson's Job

2. What does the word **caches** mean in the story?

   A. igloos built for sleeping

   B. money you carry with you

   C. special stockpiles of food or supplies

   D. a sled for traveling on the snow

3. Number the following events in the order they happened.

   ____ Robert Peary's team has to turn back because the ice around the pole melts.

   ____ Robert Peary says that he will make one more trip to the Arctic.

   ____ Matthew Henson starts working for Robert Peary.

   ____ Matthew Henson makes careful plans for the final trip to the north pole.

   ____ Matthew Henson stands at the north pole for the first time.

4. Answer the following questions.

   • What was Matthew Henson's job?

   _____

   _____

   • Who was Robert Peary?

   _____

   • Where did Henson get some of his information for trip planning?

   _____

   _____

   • How many people died trying to get to the north pole before Henson and Peary succeeded?

   _____

5. Why was Matthew Henson the first person to reach the north pole?

   A. He was the best sled driver, so he broke the trail and led the way.

   B. He was faster than everyone else.

   C. He promised himself he would be first.

   D. He left the rest of the group and found his own way.

BONUS: Write a paragraph about what it would be like to be at the north pole. What do you see? What do you feel? What does the place look like? How did you get there?

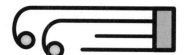

SCOTT JOPLIN
(1867?–1917)

Scott Joplin was born to make music. When he was a little boy in Texas, he learned to play the banjo. There is a story about how his mother helped to encourage Scott's music. Scott's mother cleaned houses. She asked her employers if Scott could come to their homes and play their pianos. We don't know if this story is true, but we do know that when Scott was older, he said that his mother helped him in many ways with his music. She was a singer and loved the banjo. Scott's family life was filled with music.

Scott studied with a music teacher when he was about 11 years old. The teacher, who was from Germany, gave Scott lessons for free. Scott learned about many types of music from this teacher. He learned to appreciate **opera**. An opera is like a play, but the actors sing instead of speaking their lines. Later, Scott wrote two operas of his own.

Scott went to live in St. Louis, Missouri, around 1890. It was there that he first heard about a new kind of music called ragtime. This style of piano music is lively and fun.

The left hand keeps a steady beat, while the right hand plays the song, or melody. Some ragtime pieces are based on old folk songs. Scott loved it. In 1893, a huge world's fair opened in Chicago, Illinois. Scott played at the fair with a band, sharing ragtime music with the crowds.

The fair ended, and Scott, along with his band, traveled around the country. They played their ragtime music for many people from Texas to New York. Scott started writing his own ragtime pieces during this time. He titled one of his first songs "The Maple Leaf Rag." It was first published in 1899, and the sheet music sold over one million copies.

Scott kept writing ragtime compositions, but he also tried to write more serious music. He wrote his two operas and also composed music for a ballet. He tried to pay to produce these works and present them on stage. But at the time, people liked Scott's ragtime best. Today, people still think of him as the father of this happy style of music.

SCOTT JOPLIN
(1867?–1917)

Scott Joplin was born to make music. When he was a little boy in Texas, he learned to play the banjo. There is a story about his mother and Scott's music. She cleaned houses. She asked the people who owned the houses if Scott could play their pianos. We don't know if this story is true. But, we do know that when Scott was older, he said that his mother helped him in many ways with his music. She was a singer and loved the banjo. Scott's family life was filled with music.

Scott studied with a teacher when he was about 11 years old. The teacher was German. He gave Scott lessons for free. Scott learned about many kinds of music. He learned to like **opera**. An opera is like a play. But, the actors sing instead of talking. Later, Scott wrote two operas of his own.

Scott went to live in St. Louis, Missouri, around 1890. It was there that he first heard about a new kind of music called ragtime.

This piano music is lively. The left hand keeps a steady beat. The right hand plays the song, or melody. Some ragtime pieces are based on old folk songs. Scott loved it. In 1893, a huge world's fair opened in Chicago, Illinois. Scott played at the fair with a band. He played ragtime music.

The fair ended. Scott and his band traveled around the country. They played their ragtime music for many people. Scott started to write his own ragtime pieces. He called one of his first songs "The Maple Leaf Rag." It was printed in 1899. The sheet music sold over one million copies.

Scott kept writing ragtime pieces. He also tried to write other music. He wrote his two operas. He wrote music for a ballet. He tried to pay to get these works staged. But at the time, people liked Scott's ragtime best. Today, people still think of him as the father of this happy style of music.

SCOTT JOPLIN
(1867?–1917)

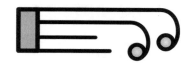

1. This story tells about:

   A. a man who learns to play the banjo.

   B. the man who made ragtime music famous.

   C. a man who got free music lessons.

   D. a man who loved only one kind of music.

2. What does the word **opera** mean in the story?

   A. a new kind of music based on folk songs

   B. a new kind of music for pianos

   C. a play in which the lines are sung instead of spoken

   D. a new kind of musical instrument

3. Number the following events in the order they happened.

   _____ Scott takes music lessons.

   _____ Scott writes a ragtime piece called "The Maple Leaf Rag."

   _____ Scott learns to play the piano.

   _____ Scott writes two operas.

   _____ Scott learns to play the banjo.

4. Answer the following questions.

   • Which instrument did Scott learn to play first?

   _____

   • Who gave Scott music lessons?

   _____

   • Where was the world's fair in 1893?

   _____

   • How might Scott's mother have helped him with his music?

   _____

   _____

5. Why do you think Scott tried to pay to get his operas and ballet staged?

   A. Nobody else would produce them, and he wanted people to see them.

   B. He wanted people to hear his new ragtime pieces.

   C. Nobody liked opera music except him.

   D. Scott wanted to own his own theater.

BONUS: What kind of music do you like? Write about that kind of music and tell why you like it.

W. E. B. DUBOIS
(1868–1963)

It was summer. William DuBois was on vacation, but he was not taking his summer off. He was planning to be a teacher. William was a college student in Tennessee. He went to the countryside and found a little school. He taught there all summer. The school was a log hut that had once been used to store corn. Now, it had rows of seats made of planks for the 30 students. This was the first time William ever taught. He told the children stories of a world far away from Tennessee. It was a world he wanted to see, too.

William graduated from college in Tennessee and went on to Harvard. He was the first black person to earn a PhD there. Then, he kept teaching. He worked at Atlanta University in Atlanta, Georgia. He liked teaching. He also wrote books based on his studies of how black people lived in the United States. William was determined to help them.

In 1900, William thought it was time for new thinking about African Americans. He helped plan a meeting called the Pan-African Conference. At this meeting, held in London, England, black people from around the world talked about their rights, their dreams, and their problems. More meetings were held. William listened to all of the ideas that were presented. He decided that a group was needed to take action and make changes on behalf of African Americans. In 1909, William helped start this new group. It was called the National Association for the Advancement of Colored People, or the NAACP.

The NAACP worked to help black people in the United States. African Americans in the South were forced to pass hard tests just to vote. William thought this was wrong. Other bad things were happening in the South. African Americans were being hurt and killed. The NAACP used the courts to fight these things. The group helped people who were being hurt and being kept from voting simply because they were black. The NAACP is still an important group today.

William's work started in a **corncrib** school. He ended up helping to lead a hard-working group that aids people across the country. In this way, he became a teacher for everyone, black and white alike.

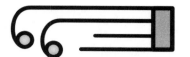
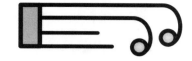

W. E. B. DUBOIS
(1868–1963)

It was summer. William DuBois was on vacation. But, he was not taking his summer off. He was going to be a teacher. William was a college student in Tennessee. He found a little school in the country. He was going to teach there during the summer. The school was in a log hut. It was once used to store corn. Now, it had rows of seats made of planks. There were 30 students. This was the first time William ever taught. He told the children stories of places far away from Tennessee. It was a world he wanted to see, too.

William finished college in Tennessee. He went to Harvard. He was the first black person to earn a PhD there. Then, he kept teaching. He taught at Atlanta University in Atlanta, Georgia. He liked teaching. He also wrote books. He studied how black people lived in the United States. He wanted to help them.

In 1900, William thought it was time for some new thinking about how to change the lives of black people. He helped plan a big meeting in London, England. It was called the Pan-African Conference. Black people came to the meeting from across the world.

They talked about their rights, their dreams, and their problems. More meetings were held. William listened to all of the ideas at these meetings. He thought that a group needed to speak for black people. In 1909, he helped start this new group. It was called the National Association for the Advancement of Colored People, or the NAACP.

The NAACP worked to help black people in the United States. Some black people in the South had to pass hard tests just to vote. William thought that was wrong. Other bad things were happening in the South, too. Black people were being hurt and killed. The NAACP used the courts. They fought to help black people who were being hurt and who were being kept from voting. The NAACP is still an important group today.

William's work started in a **corncrib** school. He ended up helping to lead a hard-working group. The group helps people across the country. In this way, he became a teacher for everyone, black and white.

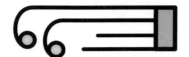

W. E. B. DUBOIS
(1868–1963)

1. The first paragraph is mainly about William's:

   A. work on the Pan-African Conference.

   B. graduation from Harvard.

   C. use of the courts to help people.

   D. first teaching job.

2. What does the word **corncrib** mean in the story?

   A. a place where farmworkers sleep

   B. a bed for a baby

   C. a small building or shed where corn is stored

   D. a farmhouse

3. Number the following events in the order they happened.

   ____ William goes to Harvard.

   ____ William goes to London for a big international meeting.

   ____ William helps start the NAACP.

   ____ William goes to college in Tennessee.

   ____ William helps plan the first Pan-African Conference in 1900.

4. Answer the following questions.

   • What is the NAACP?

   _____

   _____

   _____

   _____

   • When was the NAACP started?

   _____

   • Who were William's first students?

   _____

   • Where were African Americans having the most trouble?

   _____

5. Why did William decide to start the NAACP?

   A. He decided that a group was needed to help speak for African Americans.

   B. He wanted his own group, not the Pan-African Conference.

   C. He wanted to start a special school for black people.

   D. none of the above

BONUS: What do you think African Americans discussed at the first Pan-African Conference? Remember, slavery in the United States only ended about 40 years earlier. Do you think that black people from other countries had the same problems?

 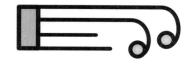

BESSIE COLEMAN
(1892–1926)

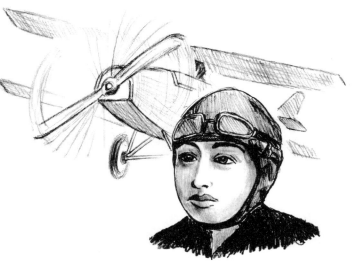

Bessie Coleman was born in Texas. Her young life was difficult. She had 12 brothers and sisters, and her father had left the family. Bessie helped make money by picking cotton. She was a talented student, but the family had no money to send Bessie to college. Bessie saved her own money, but she was only able to attend college for one term.

So, Bessie moved to Chicago, Illinois, to live with her brother Walter. Two of her brothers fought in World War I. They told Bessie about the airplanes in France. The more they talked, the more Bessie wanted to try her hand at flying. Planes were a novelty then, and few people in the United States knew how to fly. Bessie went to the flying schools in Chicago, but none of the teachers would allow her to fly. She was black, and she was a woman. Because of these two things, it appeared that Bessie's dream would just crumble.

Bessie would not let her dream fade away. She started saving her money again, and she also learned French. In 1920, Bessie took a ship to France, where she enrolled in a flying school. She learned to fly a plane. In 1921, she went home to the United States, and the next year, she started flying.

In those days, planes did not have many **practical** uses. Most of the trained pilots flew in air shows. Bessie started "barnstorming." That was the word people used for the dangerous tricks pilots did in air shows. People loved to see Bessie fly because she was so brave. She wasn't just flying for the thrills. She had a reason for flying in the shows: she was making money to open her own flying school.

Bessie thought that other black people should try this exciting new job. She gave speeches about airplanes and aviation. She also refused to fly at any show where black people were not allowed in the audience. She worked for four years to earn money to start her school.

But sadly, Bessie did not get to open her school. In 1926, she was testing a plane for a flight. In those days, the cockpit, the area where the pilot sat, was open and without any roof. During the flight, her copilot lost control of the plane. Bessie fell out of the plane and died. Today, she lives on in the history of flight as the first African American woman to become a pilot.

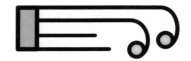

BESSIE COLEMAN
(1892–1926)

Bessie Coleman was born in Texas. Her young life was hard. She had 12 brothers and sisters. Her father left the family. Bessie helped make money by picking cotton. She was a smart student, but there was no money for her to go to college. Bessie saved her own money. She was only able to go to college for one term.

So, Bessie moved to Chicago, Illinois. She lived with her brother Walter. Two of her brothers fought in World War I. They told Bessie about the airplanes in France. The more they talked, the more Bessie wanted to try flying. Planes were new then. Bessie went to the flying schools in Chicago, but none of the teachers would let her fly. She was black. She was a woman. Because of these two things, it seemed that Bessie's dream would just die.

Bessie would not let her dream die. She started saving her money again. She learned French. In 1920, Bessie took a ship to France. She found a flying school there. She learned to fly. In 1921, she went home to the United States. The next year, she started flying.

In those days, planes did not have many **practical** uses. Lots of pilots flew in air shows. Bessie started "barnstorming." That was the word people used for the tricks pilots did in air shows. People loved to see Bessie fly. She was very brave. But, she had a reason for flying in the shows. She was making money to open her own flying school.

Bessie thought that other black people should try this exciting new job. She gave speeches about it. She also would not fly at any show where black people were not allowed in the audience. She worked for four years to earn money for her school.

But sadly, Bessie did not get to open her school. In 1926, she was testing a plane for a flight. In those days, the place where the pilot sat did not have a roof over it. During the flight, her copilot lost control of the plane. Bessie fell out of the plane and died. Today, she lives on in the history of flight. She was the first African American woman to become a pilot.

NAME: _____ DATE: _____

BESSIE COLEMAN
(1892–1926)

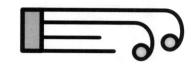

1. The second paragraph is mainly about Bessie:

   A. growing up in Texas.

   B. learning to fly in France.

   C. trying to learn to fly in Chicago.

   D. saving money to open her own school.

2. What does the word **practical** mean in the story?

   A. having a use that helps people

   B. almost

   C. used only for fun

   D. trying something over and over

3. Number the following events in the order they happened.

   _____ Bessie starts barnstorming in shows.

   _____ Bessie picks cotton to help earn money for her family.

   _____ Bessie's brothers tell her about the airplanes they saw in France.

   _____ Bessie falls out of an airplane and dies.

   _____ Bessie learns French and goes to a flying school in France.

4. Answer the following questions.

   • What was Bessie's childhood like?

   _____

   _____

   • Who was Walter?

   _____

   • Where was Bessie born?

   _____

   • When did Bessie start flying as a pilot in the United States?

   _____

5. Why did Bessie have to go to France to learn to fly?

   A. American schools would not let her fly because she was black and a woman.

   B. American schools were not any good.

   C. She had learned French and wanted to speak it.

   D. none of the above

BONUS: What would it be like to be the pilot of a plane? Write a paragraph or a poem telling about the feeling of flying.

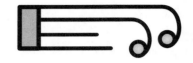

MARIAN ANDERSON
(1897–1993)

Marian Anderson was a singer with a strong, beautiful voice. She could sing very high notes and very low notes. People who heard her sing never forgot it.

Marian was born in Philadelphia, Pennsylvania. She started singing when she was very young. She sang in the choir at her church. People in her church helped raise money for Marian. The money was for music lessons. But, one music school turned her away because the school said that it would not teach a black person. Her high school principal helped Marian find a good music teacher who helped her **perfect** her voice.

Marian won a singing contest in 1925. In 1928, she gave a big concert in New York, New York. People said that she wasn't ready to sing in all of the different languages that a concert singer was required to know. So, Marian went to Europe. She studied hard.

When she had learned what she needed to know, she came home to the United States.

By this time, Marian was famous. But, she still had trouble when she traveled because she was black. At that point in history, black people were not allowed in many of the same places as white people. Sometimes, Marian could not find a restaurant that would let her have a table. She had to eat in her room instead. Sometimes, she had to stay with friends because no hotel would rent her a room.

In 1939, Marian was going to give a concert in Washington, D.C. The people who owned the hall would not let her sing there. Eleanor Roosevelt, the First Lady, heard about this. She was angry. She helped Marian plan a concert at the Lincoln Memorial on Washington Mall. Marian stood in front of the huge statue of Lincoln. She sang. Over 75,000 people came to hear her.

After that day, Marian would never again sing in a hall where black people were not welcome. She refused to give concerts unless African Americans could come to hear her. She won prize money that she gave away to help black music students. In 1963, Marian was given a medal for her work for African Americans. Her voice was a great gift to music. Her brave heart made her a leader for freedom and civil rights.

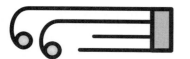 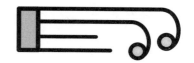

MARIAN ANDERSON
(1897–1993)

Marian Anderson was a singer. Her voice was strong and beautiful. She could sing very high notes and very low notes. People who heard her sing never forgot it.

Marian was born in Philadelphia, Pennsylvania. She started to sing when she was very young. She sang in the choir at her church. People in her church helped raise money for Marian. The money was for music lessons. But, one music school turned her away. The school said that it would not teach a black person. Her high school principal helped Marian find a good music teacher who helped her **perfect** her voice.

Marian won a singing contest in 1925. In 1928, she gave a big concert in New York, New York. People said that she wasn't ready. She needed to learn different languages. Then, she could sing songs that were not in English. So, Marian went to Europe. She studied hard. She learned what she needed to know. Then, she came home.

By this time, Marian was well-known. But, she still had trouble when she traveled. At that time, black people were not allowed in many of the same places as white people. Sometimes, Marian could not find a place where she could eat. She had to eat in her room instead. Sometimes, she had to stay with friends. No hotel would rent her a room.

Marian was going to give a concert in Washington, D.C., in 1939. The people who owned the hall would not let her sing there. The First Lady, Eleanor Roosevelt, heard about this. She was angry. She helped Marian plan a concert outside. Marian stood in front of the Lincoln Memorial on the Washington Mall. She sang. Over 75,000 people came to hear her.

Marian would never again sing in a hall where black people were not welcome. She won prize money. She gave it away to help black music students. She was given a medal for her work for African Americans. Her voice was a great gift to music. Her brave heart was a gift, too. She was a leader for freedom and civil rights.

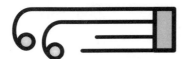 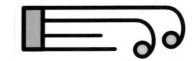

MARIAN ANDERSON
(1897–1993)

1. What is the main idea of the fourth paragraph?

   A. Marian's childhood

   B. the medal Marian won

   C. the trouble Marian had when she traveled

   D. Marian's voice

2. What does the word **perfect** mean in the story?

   A. without flaws

   B. make-believe

   C. to work on something until it is polished or improved

   D. deep and thoughtful

3. Number the following events in the order they happened.

   _____ Marian wins a singing contest.

   _____ Marian travels to Europe to learn different languages.

   _____ Marian sings in a church choir.

   _____ Marian gives away prize money to help music students.

   _____ Marian is not allowed to sing in a concert hall in Washington, D.C.

4. Answer the following questions.

   • What talent was Marian Anderson famous for?

   _____

   • Who helped Marian plan an outdoor concert in Washington, D.C.?

   _____

   • Where was the concert in Washington, D.C., held?

   _____

   • What was one way that Marian helped other African Americans?

   _____

   _____

5. Why did Marian have trouble finding places to eat and stay when she went on trips?

   A. She was very picky about where she stayed and what she ate.

   B. She did not like to travel.

   C. She was black, and at that time, black people were not allowed to go to many places where white people could go.

   D. She was so famous that people bothered her in restaurants and hotels.

BONUS: The Lincoln Memorial, where Marian sang, is only one of many places in Washington, D.C. Read or think about other places in Washington, D.C. Which place would you most like to visit? Why?

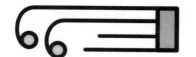 

LOUIS ARMSTRONG
(1901–1971)

Louis Armstrong's young life was not a promising one. Louis was born in New Orleans, Louisiana. His family was very poor, and he danced for pennies that he used to buy food. The year he turned 12, he was celebrating at a party on New Year's Eve. He fired a pistol into the air at midnight as a noisemaker. The police took him into custody and sent him to a state home for boys. Who could have guessed this would be the start of a renowned life in music?

At the home was a music teacher named Peter Davis. Peter offered to work with Louis. He taught the boy to sing and showed him how to play the trumpet. Louis also attended school while he was at the home. When Louis left the home for boys, he knew something he hadn't known before: how to make music. He started playing with a band on the big riverboats that went up and down the Mississippi River.

A bandleader named King Oliver befriended Louis, and Louis moved to Chicago, Illinois, to play in his band. The band played jazz, a favorite style of music in New Orleans. Louis was so talented at creating the beat and rhythm of jazz that soon he had a band of his own. Louis's band played songs that were popular at the time, but when he played them, the songs sounded **unique**. People started coming just to hear Louis play and sing.

Louis loved to travel. He went to California to play music. He traveled to New York, New York. He went back to New Orleans to play for his old fans. He also toured in Europe and Africa. Everywhere he went, people loved his music. Louis played for both kings and the common people. He made recordings of his music for 50 years. He acted in 30 movies. He also wrote two memoirs about his life and experiences.

One of the things everyone loved about Louis was his huge, happy smile. They loved his jokes and the simple way he lived. But most of all, people loved Louis's music. People still listen to recordings of his music today. He had a beat and a style that were like no one else's.

LOUIS ARMSTRONG
(1901–1971)

ouis Armstrong's young life was not a promising one. Louis was born in New Orleans, Louisiana. His family was very poor. He danced for pennies that he used to buy food. When he was 12 years old, he was at a party on New Year's Eve. He fired a gun into the air at midnight to make noise. The police took him to a state home for boys. Who could have guessed this would be the start of a long, famous life in music?

At the home was a music teacher. His name was Peter Davis. Peter worked with Louis. He taught the boy to sing. He showed him how to play the trumpet. Louis also attended school while he was at the home. Then, Louis left the boys' home. When he left, he knew how to do something new: make music. He started playing with a band on the big riverboats that went up and down the Mississippi River.

A bandleader named King Oliver became Louis's friend. Louis moved to Chicago, Illinois, to play in his band. The band played jazz. Jazz was a favorite type of music in New Orleans. Louis was so good at this style of music that soon he had his own band. Louis played songs that were popular at the time. But when he played the songs, they sounded **unique**. People started coming just to hear Louis play and sing.

Louis loved to travel. He went to California to play music. He went to New York, New York. He went back to New Orleans to play for his fans there. He traveled to Europe and Africa. Louis played music for both kings and the common people. He made records of his music for 50 years. He acted in 30 movies. He also wrote two books about his life and memories.

One of the things everyone loved about Louis was his huge, happy smile. They loved his jokes. They loved the simple way he lived. But most of all, they loved Louis's music. People still play his music today. He had a beat and a style that were like no one else's.

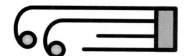

LOUIS ARMSTRONG
(1901–1971)

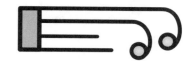

1. The second paragraph is mainly about Louis when he:

   A. played for kings in Europe.

   B. danced in the street for money.

   C. started playing in a band.

   D. learned music at a state home for boys.

2. What does the word **unique** mean in the story?

   A. unlike anything or anyone else

   B. nearly the same

   C. uninteresting

   D. strange sounding

3. Number the following events in the order they happened.

   _____ Louis goes to Europe and Africa.

   _____ Peter Davis teaches Louis to play the trumpet.

   _____ Louis moves to Chicago, Illinois, to play in King Oliver's band.

   _____ Louis finds a job playing on riverboats.

   _____ Louis goes to a New Year's Eve party and gets in trouble.

4. Answer the following questions.

   • What style of music did Louis play in his bands?

   _____

   • Who was King Oliver?

   _____

   _____

   • Where was Louis born?

   _____

   • How many movies did Louis act in?

   _____

5. Why did it turn out to be a good thing when Louis was taken to a state home for boys?

   A. He went to school at the home.

   B. He was poor, and people took care of him at the home.

   C. He learned to play music and sing at the home.

   D. all of the above

BONUS: Have you ever wanted to play a musical instrument? Which one? Write about why you want to play that instrument.

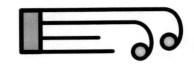

LANGSTON HUGHES
(1902–1967)

The young man stood on the deck of the ship, watching as it steamed away from New York, New York. Suddenly, he threw his books into the waves of the harbor. He was going to Africa, and he wanted to leave his past behind. It was 1923.

The man was Langston Hughes. Growing up, Langston lived in many different places. When he was in the eighth grade, he was voted "Class Poet." However, his father did not think that writing was a practical way to make money, so he sent Langston to college in New York. He wanted his son to be an engineer who helped build skyscrapers and bridges.

Langston wanted to create poems. He had already published poems in several magazines. Now, Langston wanted to see the world. He traveled around Africa. He went to Europe. When he came home, he finished his college degree. Then, he traveled to Haiti and the Soviet Union.

One of Langston's favorite places was Harlem, a section of New York City. At that time, many African American people lived there, people who were writing stories and poems and playing jazz. Langston loved to listen to the rhythm and beat of jazz music. He started using the beat of the music for the words in his poems. He said that it is the music of a people who always keep going.

Langston also wrote articles. In them, he talked about what it was like to be an African American. He was proud of his race. He wrote that black people were beautiful and should never try to be like white people. Some of his writing was printed in a magazine managed by W. E. B. DuBois. Langston always wrote with African Americans in mind. He specifically wanted them to understand his ideas and his poems.

People still read Langston's poems today. He published many books of poetry. He also wrote plays, a novel, stories, an opera, and his **autobiography**. This great writer had many interesting things to say. But, his most important message was that black people are strong and wonderful.

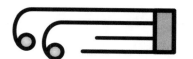

LANGSTON HUGHES
(1902–1967)

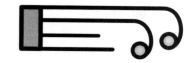

The young man stood on the deck of the ship. He watched as it steamed away from New York City, New York. Suddenly, he threw his books into the water. He was going to Africa. He was leaving his past behind. It was 1923.

The man was Langston Hughes. Langston lived in many different places growing up. When he was in the eighth grade, he was voted "Class Poet." His father did not think that writing was a good way to make money. He sent Langston to college in New York. He wanted his son to build buildings and bridges.

Langston wanted to write poems. He had already printed poems in some magazines. Now, Langston wanted to see the world. He traveled around Africa. He also went to Europe. When he came home, he finished his college classes. Then, he went to Haiti and the Soviet Union.

One of Langston's favorite places was Harlem. Harlem is a part of New York City. At that time, many black people lived there. People were writing stories and poems there. They were playing jazz. Langston loved to listen to jazz music. He started using the beat of the music in his poems. He said that jazz is the music of a people who always keep going.

Langston also wrote essays. He talked in his essays about what it was like to be a black person. He was proud of his race. He wrote that black people were beautiful. He did not think they should try to be like white people. Some of his writing was printed in a magazine put out by W. E. B. DuBois. Langston always wrote for black people. He wanted them to understand his ideas and his poems.

People still read Langston's poems today. He wrote many books of poetry. He also wrote plays, stories, and his **autobiography**. This great writer had many interesting things to say. But, his biggest message was that black people are strong and wonderful.

LANGSTON HUGHES
(1902–1967)

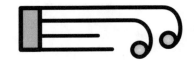

1. Choose a good title for this story.

   A. A Trip to Africa

   B. A Poet for His People

   C. Jazz and Poetry

   D. Langston's College Years

2. What does the word **autobiography** mean in the story?

   A. a life story written by another author

   B. a type of long poem

   C. a life story written by the person who lived the life

   D. a jazz music piece

3. Number the following events in the order they happened.

   ____ Langston is voted "Class Poet."

   ____ Langston goes to Africa.

   ____ Langston writes essays about being black.

   ____ Langston finished his college classes.

   ____ Langston travels to Europe.

4. Answer the following questions.

   • What did Langston's father want him to do for a living?

   _____

   • Who voted to make Langston "Class Poet"?

   _____

   • Where is Harlem?

   _____

   • How did Langston use jazz music for his poems?

   _____

   _____

5. Why did Langston always keep African Americans in mind when he wrote?

   A. He wanted them to come to Harlem and listen to music there.

   B. He wanted them to understand his feeling that black people should be proud.

   C. He wanted them to buy his books so that he could make a lot of money.

   D. He wanted them to learn more about his life so that they could write poetry, too.

BONUS: Listen to or think of a song that you like. Then, try to write a poem that fits the beat of that song.

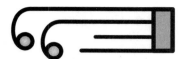

THURGOOD MARSHALL
(1908–1993)

Thurgood Marshall attended law school. When he was finished, he was asked if he would like to go to Harvard. He could get another degree there, and his entire course of study would be paid for. Thurgood said no. Why? Because he wanted to start helping African Americans as soon as he possibly could.

Thurgood became a lawyer for the National Association for the Advancement of Colored People (NAACP) in 1936. He took cases in which black people were accused of things they did not do. He also worked on cases to change laws and **integrate** schools. He wanted all schools to be open to both black students and white students.

Sometimes, Thurgood's work was dangerous. He made people angry when he spoke for African Americans and their rights. One time, an angry mob chased him. Another time, he was arrested and taken to jail for no reason. But, Thurgood refused to give up his work. He kept taking cases to court. In 1954, the Supreme Court, which is the highest court in the country, ruled on a case about an African American girl who was not allowed to attend an all-white school near her home. Thurgood told the judge that schools kept apart by race could never be considered equal. He said, "Equal means getting the same thing, at the same time, and in the same place." He won the case and changed the law.

For some people, this would have been a big enough accomplishment for an entire lifetime. It was not big enough for Thurgood Marshall. Next, he became a judge. From his bench, he kept hearing cases about civil rights. After that, he worked for the White House. Then, in 1967, he was asked to be a justice on the Supreme Court. He was the first black person to serve on the Court.

Thurgood Marshall served on the Supreme Court until 1991. He heard many cases. He spoke plainly and simply. His legal rulings helped people across the country, and the laws he helped to forge are still at work for people today.

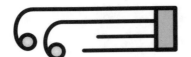
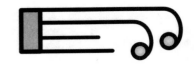
Thurgood Marshall went to law school. When he was finished, he was asked if he would like to go to Harvard. He could get another degree there. All of his classes would be paid for. Thurgood said no. Why? Because he wanted to start helping African Americans as soon as he could.

Thurgood became a lawyer for the National Association for the Advancement of Colored People (NAACP) in 1936. He took cases in which black people had been blamed for things they did not do. He also worked on cases to help **integrate** schools. He wanted all schools to be open to both black students and white students.

Sometimes, Thurgood's work was filled with danger. He made people angry when he spoke for black people. One time, an angry crowd chased him. Another time, he was taken to jail for no reason. But, Thurgood would not give up his work. He kept taking cases to court. In 1954, the Supreme Court (the highest court in the country) ruled on a case about a black girl who could not go to an all-white school near her home. Thurgood told the judge that schools kept apart by race could not be equal. He said, "Equal means getting the same thing, at the same time, and in the same place." He won. This case changed the law.

For some people, this would have been enough work for a whole lifetime. It was not enough work for Thurgood Marshall. Next, he became a judge. From his bench, he kept hearing cases about civil rights. After that, he worked for the White House. Then, in 1967, he was asked to be a justice on the Supreme Court. He was the first black person to serve on the Court.

Thurgood Marshall served on the Supreme Court until 1991. He heard many cases. He spoke plainly and simply. His work helped people all over the country. The laws he helped to make are still at work for people today.

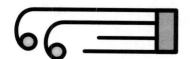

THURGOOD MARSHALL
(1908–1993)

1. This story tells about:

   A. a lawyer who fought for civil rights.

   B. an African American who went to law school.

   C. the first African American justice on the Supreme Court.

   D. all of the above

2. What does the word **integrate** mean in the story?

   A. keep places separated but equal

   B. bring together people of all races

   C. something made out of one piece of material

   D. very smart

3. Number the following events in the order they happened.

   _____ Thurgood wins a big case about equality in the schools.

   _____ Thurgood works at the White House.

   _____ Thurgood Marshall graduates from law school.

   _____ Thurgood starts working for the NAACP.

   _____ Thurgood Marshall is made a Supreme Court justice.

4. Answer the following questions.

   • What is the Supreme Court?

   _____

   _____

   • Starting in 1936, who did Thurgood Marshall work for?

   _____

   • Where could Thurgood have gone after law school if he wanted?

   _____

   • How many black Supreme Court justices were there before Thurgood Marshall?

   _____

5. Why did Thurgood want to help integrate schools?

   A. He did not believe that black students should go to school with white students.

   B. He thought that separate schools could be equal.

   C. He wanted schools to teach children the basic classes.

   D. He thought that all schools should be open to students of all races.

BONUS: What kind of job do you think you might like to do to help other people? Write a paragraph describing this job.

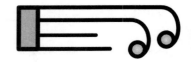

JESSE OWENS
(1913–1980)

When he was in high school, Jesse Owens realized that he loved to run. His family had moved to Cleveland, Ohio, so that his father could find a better job, but he couldn't find decent employment. Jesse had to work to help his family. A **track** coach wanted to train Jesse, but the boy had a job after school. The coach, Mr. Riley, said that he would come early in the morning to help Jesse train. He knew that Jesse would be a great runner.

Jesse became the star of the team and then went to college. He chose to attend Ohio State University in 1933. Because he was black, Jesse had to live off campus with other black athletes. When the team traveled to meets, he could only sleep at hotels that allowed black people.

In 1935, the team went to Ann Arbor, Michigan, for a big track meet. The week before the meet, Jesse fell down some stairs and hurt his back. That wasn't enough to stop him. He convinced his coach to let him run. On that day, Jesse broke three world records! He accomplished this amazing feat in less than one hour.

It was clear that Jesse should be on the Olympic team. The next year, Jesse went to Berlin, Germany, where the Olympics were being held. Hitler had risen to power in Germany. He believed that white people were superior to

every other race. He wanted the German team to prove this to the rest of the world. But, because of Jesse, things went very differently.

Jesse won three individual events. He was also on the winning team of a relay race. Soon, even the Germans were cheering for this amazing young black man. Jesse won four gold medals, the first American to do so.

When he returned home, though, Jesse's family was still struggling. Jesse left college to help earn money for them. He still ran in sporting events and gave lectures about his sporting career. Then, he started his own company, traveling and speaking for companies like Ford Motor Company. He also raised money for the Olympic Committee. In 1976, President Gerald Ford gave Jesse the Medal of Freedom, the highest award possible for a nonmilitary citizen. But, that was just one high point in Jesse's amazing life.

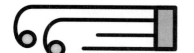

JESSE OWENS
(1913–1980)

When he was in high school, Jesse Owens loved to run. His family had moved to Cleveland, Ohio, so that his father could find a better job. But, he could not find a good job. Jesse had to work to help his family. A **track** coach wanted to train Jesse for the team. Jesse had a job after school. The coach, Mr. Riley, said that he would come early in the morning to help Jesse. He knew that Jesse would be a great runner.

Jesse became the star of the team. Then, he went to college. He went to Ohio State in 1933. Because he was black, Jesse had to live off campus with other black athletes. When the team went away to meets, he could only sleep at hotels that let black people stay there.

In 1935, the team went to Ann Arbor, Michigan, for a big meet. The week before the meet, Jesse fell down some stairs. He was hurt. That did not stop him. He begged his coach to let him run. On that day, Jesse broke three world records! He did this in less than one hour.

It was clear that Jesse should be on the Olympic team. The next year, Jesse went to Berlin, Germany. That is where the Olympics were being held. Hitler was in charge of Germany. He thought that white people were better than every other race. He wanted the German team to show this to the rest of the world. Because of Jesse, things went very differently.

Jesse won three individual events. He was also on the winning team of a relay race. Soon, even the Germans were cheering for this amazing young black man. Jesse won four gold medals. He was the first American to do this.

When he returned home, though, his family was still struggling. Jesse left college to help earn money for them. He still ran in sporting events. He gave speeches. Then, he started his own company. He traveled and spoke for companies like Ford Motor Company. He raised money for the Olympic Committee. In 1976, President Gerald Ford gave Jesse the Medal of Freedom. This is the highest award given to Americans who aren't in the military. That was just one high point in Jesse's amazing life.

JESSE OWENS
(1913–1980)

1. Which word best describes Jesse Owens?

   A. slow

   B. unhappy

   C. quiet

   D. fast

2. What does the word **track** mean in the story?

   A. a path or road

   B. a sport where people shoot at targets

   C. to follow someone or something

   D. a sport of running and jumping

3. Number the following events in the order they happened.

   _____ Jesse's family moves to Cleveland.

   _____ Jesse goes to Ohio State.

   _____ Jesse is given the Medal of Freedom.

   _____ Coach Riley starts to train Jesse.

   _____ Jesse wins four gold medals in the 1936 Olympics.

4. Answer the following questions.

   • What did Jesse do at a college track meet in Michigan?

   _____

   _____

   • Who was Hitler?

   _____

   • Where were the 1936 Olympics held?

   _____

   • How did Jesse earn a living after he was in the Olympics?

   _____

   _____

5. How did Jesse ruin Hitler's plan?

   A. Hitler wanted everyone to see how fast Jesse could run, and he lost.

   B. Jesse refused to run at the Olympics because Hitler was in power.

   C. Hitler wanted to show at the Olympics that white people were the best at sports, and Jesse was black.

   D. Hitler wanted everyone to think that the American track team was the best.

BONUS: Write a paragraph about a sport you like to play or watch. Explain the rules of the game and why you think the sport is so fun.

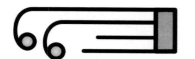 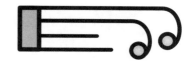

ROSA PARKS
(1913–2005)

Rosa Parks grew up on her grandparents' farm in Alabama. After going to school, Rosa went to live in the city of Montgomery. She got married and found a job as a seamstress, a person who sews clothing. Rosa and her husband joined the National Association for the Advancement of Colored People (NAACP) because they wanted to make life better for black people.

Life for African Americans was hard in the city of Montgomery. Everything was kept segregated for black people. The bus system was just one example. When black people rode a bus, they had to sit in a section in the back. If a white person demanded a black person's seat, the black person had to stand up and give away the seat.

On the night of December 1, 1955, Rosa was riding a bus home from work. She was tired from her long day. But, more than that, she was also tired of being treated as a lesser person. The white section of the bus was full. When a white man told Rosa to give up her seat, Rosa refused to stand up and give away her seat.

The bus driver called the police. Rosa was arrested. The next day, a new group was formed in Montgomery to start a **boycott** of the buses. All of the black people and some of the white people agreed not to pay to ride the buses until the rules were changed and black customers were treated the same way as white customers. Rosa helped with this boycott. The group was led by Dr. Martin Luther King, Jr.

The boycott lasted more than one year. Meanwhile, Rosa's case went all of the way to the highest court in the nation, the Supreme Court. The Supreme Court ruled that Montgomery's bus laws were wrong. Rosa had changed life in Montgomery forever with her simple wish to be treated as an equal. But more importantly, her brave act made life better for people across the country.

ROSA PARKS
(1913–2005)

Rosa Parks lived in Alabama. She grew up on her grandparents' farm. Rosa went to school. Then, she went to live in the city of Montgomery. She got married. She found a job sewing clothing. Rosa and her husband joined the National Association for the Advancement of Colored People (NAACP). They wanted to make life better for black people.

Life for black people in the city was hard. Black people could ride on the buses. But, they had to sit in the back. Sometimes, a white person wanted a black person's seat. The black person had to stand up. He had to give away his seat.

That is the way it was until the night of December 1, 1955. Rosa was riding a bus home from work. She was tired from her long day. But, she was also tired of being treated as a lesser person. The white part of the bus was full. A white man told Rosa to give up her seat. Rosa would not stand up.

The bus driver called the police. Rosa was arrested. The next day, a new group was formed in Montgomery. This group started a **boycott** of the buses. All of the black people and some of the white people said that they would not ride the buses. They would not pay for bus rides until black people were treated the same way as white people. Rosa helped with this boycott. The group was led by Dr. Martin Luther King, Jr.

The boycott lasted more than one year. Rosa's case went all of the way to the highest court in the country, the Supreme Court. The Supreme Court ruled that Montgomery's bus laws were wrong. Rosa changed life in Montgomery forever with her simple wish to be treated as an equal. Her brave act also made life better for people across the country.

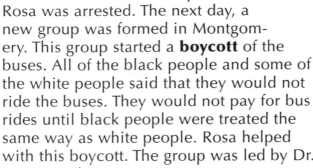

ROSA PARKS
(1913–2005)

1. This story tells about:

   A. Rosa Parks's childhood.

   B. how Rosa Parks boycotted the buses in Arkansas.

   C. how Rosa Parks fought for civil rights in Alabama.

   D. how Rosa Parks earned a living.

2. What does the word **boycott** mean in the story?

   A. not buying a service or thing until a wrong is righted

   B. getting a big group of people to buy or use something to help earn money

   C. drawing or painting designs on something

   D. paying to have something fixed

3. Number the following events in the order they happened.

   _____ Rosa will not give up her seat on a bus to a white man.

   _____ Rosa moves to Montgomery and gets a job.

   _____ African Americans in Montgomery refuse to ride the buses.

   _____ The Supreme Court says that the Montgomery bus laws are wrong.

   _____ Rosa grows up on a farm.

4. Answer the following questions.

   • What law did Rosa Parks not obey on December 1, 1955?

   _____

   _____

   • Who was the leader of the bus boycott?

   _____

   • Where did Rosa Parks live in 1955?

   _____

   • How were the bus laws finally changed?

   _____

   _____

5. Why did Rosa refuse to give up her seat on the bus?

   A. She wanted to help change the laws about buses.

   B. She wanted to be treated the same way as white people.

   C. She wanted to help other African Americans in Alabama.

   D. all of the above

BONUS: Have you ever felt that something was not fair? What did you do? Write a story describing what was unfair and how you acted.

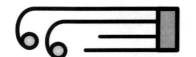
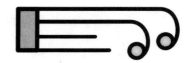

DAISY BATES
(1914?–1999)

Daisy Bates and her husband, L. C. Bates, married in 1941 and moved to Little Rock, Arkansas. Her husband started a newspaper there called the *Arkansas State Press*. The next year, in 1942, Daisy started working with her husband at the paper. Their newspaper bravely told stories of wrongs done to black people. It showed how black soldiers at a camp nearby were **mistreated**. The paper also ran stories about problems with the police. White people who owned stores would not run ads in the paper. Still, Daisy and her husband kept writing the stories and printing the paper.

Daisy and her husband were both members of the National Association for the Advancement of Colored People (NAACP). In 1952, Daisy was made president of the NAACP in Arkansas. In 1954, the Supreme Court ruled that all schools had to be open to all students. States could no longer keep black students out of white schools.

Daisy knew there was going to be trouble in Arkansas with this new law. She chose to be a leader and help black students as they tried to enter segregated schools. She took black students to school, making sure that reporters were there to take pictures. Sometimes, the students were told that they could not even enter the schools. Then, Daisy and her husband would write stories about it in their newspaper.

Central High School was the main high school in Little Rock, Arkansas. In 1957, the school board said that the school had to admit black students. Daisy helped select nine students and told them that she would help them every step of the way. On the night before school started, the nine students met at Daisy's house. Daisy and her husband talked to the students and told them about the trials they would face. The next day, Daisy went to school with them. There were huge crowds of angry people. The principal would not let the nine black students enter the school. Daisy and the students tried again the next day and the day after that.

Finally, the president of the United States had to send troops to Little Rock. One thousand soldiers guarded the students as they walked into the school. Daisy kept in touch with the students every day because attending the school was difficult. The school was even closed for a while in an effort to discourage the nine black students. Daisy and her "Little Rock Nine" remained strong. They helped all students with their brave efforts to go to Central High School.

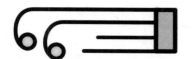 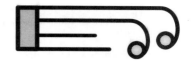

DAISY BATES
(1914?–1999)

Daisy Bates and her husband, L. C. Bates, married in 1941. They moved to Little Rock, Arkansas. Daisy's husband started a newspaper that same year. It was called the *Arkansas State Press*. Daisy started running the paper with her husband the next year. Their newspaper told stories of wrongs done to black people. It showed how black soldiers at a camp nearby were **mistreated**. The paper ran stories about trouble with the police. White people who owned stores would not print ads in the paper. Still, Daisy and her husband kept writing the stories and printing the newspaper.

Daisy and her husband were both members of the National Association for the Advancement of Colored People (NAACP). In 1952, Daisy was made president of the NAACP in Arkansas. In 1954, the Supreme Court said that all schools had to be open to all students. States could not keep black students out of white schools.

Daisy knew there was going to be trouble in her state because of this new law. She chose to help black students. She took black students to school. She made sure that reporters were there to take pictures. Sometimes, the students were told that they could not enter the schools. Then, Daisy and her husband would write stories about it in their newspaper.

Central High School was the main high school in Little Rock. In 1957, the school had to start admitting black students. Daisy helped pick nine students. She told them that she would help them every step of the way. On the night before school started, these nine students met at Daisy's house. Daisy and her husband talked to the students. They told them what they would face. The next day, Daisy went to school with the students. There were huge, angry crowds. The principal would not let the nine black students inside. Daisy and the students tried again the next day. They tried the day after that, too.

The president of the United States had to send troops to Little Rock. One thousand soldiers kept the students safe as they walked into the school. Daisy talked to the students every day. Going to the school was hard. The school even closed for a while to try to stop the nine black students from coming. Daisy and her "Little Rock Nine" stayed strong. They helped all students with their brave stand at Central High School.

DAISY BATES
(1914?–1999)

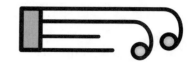

1. The first paragraph is mainly about Daisy:

   A. helping students in Little Rock schools.

   B. taking nine students to Central High School.

   C. getting married and running a newspaper.

   D. assigning reporters to take pictures.

2. What does the word **mistreated** mean in the story?

   A. treated well

   B. treated fairly

   C. treated badly

   D. treated humorously

3. Number the following events in the order they happened.

   _____ Daisy and her husband start running a newspaper together.

   _____ Daisy helps the "Little Rock Nine."

   _____ Daisy and her husband move to Little Rock, Arkansas.

   _____ The Supreme Court changes laws about schools.

   _____ Daisy becomes president of the Arkansas NAACP.

4. Answer the following questions.

   • What was Daisy's newspaper called?

   _____

   • Who did Daisy help at Central High School?

   _____

   _____

   • When did Daisy's husband start a newspaper?

   _____

   • How did Daisy help change schools in Little Rock?

   _____

   _____

   _____

5. What was the MOST important thing about Daisy's work with the "Little Rock Nine"?

   A. She helped the students get into school and helped them face problems there.

   B. She had reporters take pictures.

   C. She was president of the NAACP in the state.

   D. She was there to talk to reporters.

BONUS: Think about how hard it must have been for those nine students to go to a school where they were not wanted. Pretend you were one of the students. Write a paragraph about how you felt on the night before your first day at school.

GWENDOLYN BROOKS
(1917–2000)

The little girl started writing poems when she was seven years old. Her parents saw how she loved to work with words, so they encouraged her. They set up a desk and told her she could write instead of doing household chores.

Gwendolyn Brooks's family was poor, but they felt rich in each other's company. Later in her life, Gwendolyn wrote about families like her own. The people in her poems lived in the city. They did not have very much, and sometimes, they did not have enough to eat. But, they loved life.

By the time she was 16 years old, Gwendolyn had published 75 of her poems. When she was 25, she won her first writing award. Two years later, in 1945, her first book of poems was released. Gwendolyn wrote about the part of Chicago, Illinois, where she lived. This area is called the South Side. The poems tell stories about different people who lived in the neighborhood. People liked her book very much.

Four years later, in 1949, Gwendolyn published another book of poems. This book was called *Annie Allen*. It won the most important writing award in the United States, the Pulitzer Prize. Gwendolyn was the first African American to win this award.

After winning the Pulitzer Prize, people asked Gwendolyn to teach writing. She taught at colleges and also led small groups of writing students. Gwendolyn also worked for the Library of Congress, the largest library in the United States. Gwendolyn helped the library answer questions about poetry.

Gwendolyn kept writing. Some of her poems are about the brave work that was done for civil rights, and she wrote about the difficult life faced by black people in the South. Gwendolyn also kept writing about the life she saw around her in the city. She once said that she was like a **reporter** for a newspaper. She had to keep telling people about the things she saw going on around her every day.

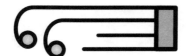
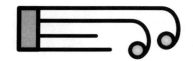

GWENDOLYN BROOKS
(1917–2000)

The little girl started writing poems when she was seven years old. Her parents saw how she loved to work with words. They set up a desk for her. They told her she could write instead of doing chores in the house.

Gwendolyn Brooks' family was poor. But, they felt rich because they were happy. Later in her life, Gwendolyn wrote about families like hers. These people lived in the city. They did not have very much. Sometimes, they did not have enough to eat. But, they loved life.

By the time Gwendolyn was 16, she had 75 poems in print. She won her first writing award when she was 25. Two years later, in 1945, her first book of poems was published. Gwendolyn wrote about the part of Chicago, Illinois, where she lived. The poems tell stories about people who lived in her neighborhood. People liked her book very much.

In 1949, Gwendolyn published another book of poems. This book was called *Annie Allen*. It won the most important writing prize in the United States. It is called the Pulitzer Prize. Gwendolyn was the first black person to win this prize.

After that, people asked Gwendolyn to teach writing. She taught at colleges. She taught small groups of writing students. Gwendolyn also worked for the Library of Congress. It is the biggest library in the United States. Gwendolyn helped the library answer questions about poetry.

Gwendolyn kept writing. Some of her poems are about the brave work that was done for equal rights. She wrote about the lives of black people in the South. Gwendolyn also kept writing about the life she saw around her in the city. She said that she was like a **reporter** for a newspaper. She had to keep telling people about the things she saw going on around her.

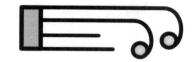

GWENDOLYN BROOKS
(1917–2000)

1. What is the main idea of the third paragraph?

   A. how Gwendolyn's parents helped her write

   B. how Gwendolyn taught writing classes

   C. how Gwendolyn's talent was seen when she was young

   D. how Gwendolyn felt about writing

2. What does the word **reporter** mean in the story?

   A. someone who writes reports for school

   B. someone who writes poems for a living

   C. someone who adds numbers for taxes

   D. someone who writes news stories for a newspaper or magazine

3. Number the following events in the order they happened.

   ____ Gwendolyn has 75 poems in print.

   ____ Gwendolyn writes *Annie Allen*.

   ____ Gwendolyn's parents set up a desk for her so that she can write.

   ____ Gwendolyn's first book of poems comes out.

   ____ Gwendolyn works for the Library of Congress.

4. Answer the following questions.

   • What big award did Gwendolyn win?

   _____

   • Who did Gwendolyn write about in most of her poems?

   _____

   • When did Gwendolyn write her first poem?

   _____

   • When did Gwendolyn write her second book of poems?

   _____

5. Why was it especially important that Gwendolyn won the Pulitzer Prize?

   A. She was the first person to win the award.

   B. She was the first poet to win the award.

   C. She was the first woman to win the award.

   D. She was the first African American to win the award.

BONUS: What kind of poem could you write about your family or your neighborhood? Make a list of words that you would use in your poem. Then, write the poem.

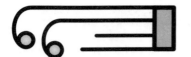

JACOB LAWRENCE
(1917–2000)

Jacob Lawrence moved to Harlem with his mother when he was 13 years old. Harlem is a section of New York, New York, and it was a special place at that time. Many black people lived there; they were creative people who were making art and music. Jacob loved it. He went to a special school where the teachers helped him learn to paint and draw.

Jacob also loved going to the big **museums** in New York City. He gazed at paintings. He studied masks and other objects from Africa. He got many ideas from looking at the art in the museums. He also got many ideas from looking at life around him. He loved to watch people walking down the street. He loved the bright store windows. He loved the busy streets. Many of his first paintings show lively city scenes like this.

Some of Jacob's next paintings displayed stories from the history of black people. He painted pictures of slaves escaping on Underground Railroad routes. He painted a well-known picture of Harriet Tubman helping slaves escape. He painted portraits of brave people like Frederick Douglass.

Jacob also wanted to tell the stories of people who were not famous. So, he started working on a big idea: a group of paintings that showed how black people left farms in the South and migrated to the North to look for jobs. Jacob painted 60 pictures to tell this story! The series was called *The Migration* and became very famous.

Today, you can see Jacob's work in many museums around the world. Each one of his bright, beautiful paintings tells a special story.

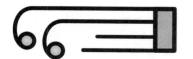 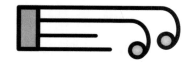

JACOB LAWRENCE
(1917–2000)

Jacob Lawrence was 13 years old when he moved to Harlem. He moved there with his mother. Harlem is a part of New York, New York. It was a special place at that time. Many black people lived there. They were making art and music. Jacob loved it. He went to a good school. The teachers helped him learn to paint and draw.

Jacob also loved going to the big **museums** in New York City. He looked at paintings. He looked at masks and other art from Africa. He got many ideas from looking at the art in the museums. He also got many ideas from looking at life around him. He loved to watch people walking down the street. He loved the bright store windows. He loved the busy streets. Many of his first paintings show city scenes like this.

Then, Jacob made paintings about black people. He showed their history. He painted pictures of slaves on the Underground Railroad. He painted a well-known picture of Harriet Tubman helping slaves run away. He showed brave people like Frederick Douglass in his pictures.

Jacob also wanted to tell the stories of regular people. He started working on a big idea. He wanted to make a whole group of paintings that told one story. These paintings would show how black people lived on farms in the South. Then, they left their farms. They went to the North to look for jobs. He wanted to show how hard this was for them. Jacob painted 60 paintings to tell this story! The series was called *The Migration*.

You can find Jacob's paintings in many museums today. People around the world study his work. Each one of his bright, beautiful paintings tells a story.

JACOB LAWRENCE
(1917–2000)

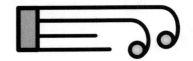

1. What is the main idea of the second paragraph?

   A. how Jacob got ideas for his paintings

   B. how Jacob moved to Harlem

   C. how Jacob painted historical pictures

   D. how Jacob made a living

2. What does the word **museums** mean in the story?

   A. places where you can buy paintings

   B. places where you can play sports

   C. places where you can buy dinner

   D. places where you can look at paintings and other objects

3. Number the following events in the order they happened.

   ____ Jacob creates paintings about the Underground Railroad.

   ____ Jacob paints a big group of pictures to tell one story.

   ____ Jacob and his mother move to New York City.

   ____ Jacob goes to museums to look at art.

   ____ Jacob starts painting the history of black people.

4. Answer the following questions.

   • What did Jacob study when he went to school?

   _____

   • Who did Jacob paint famous pictures of?

   _____

   • Where did Jacob live?

   _____

   • How did Jacob get ideas for his paintings?

   _____

   _____

5. Why did Jacob create 60 paintings about one thing?

   A. He wanted to tell a big story about black people moving north in the United States.

   B. He wanted to sell lots of paintings to black people who had moved.

   C. He wanted to show how white people came to America.

   D. none of the above

BONUS: If you could paint pictures about anything, what would you like to paint? Why? Tell about a painting you would create.

 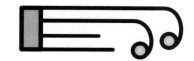

JACKIE ROBINSON
(1919–1972)

It was clear from the start that Jackie Robinson was a great athlete. He went to college at UCLA, and while he was there, he won letters in four sports: baseball, basketball, football, and track.

At the time Jackie was growing up, teams were **segregated**. That meant that only white players were allowed to play on professional teams. Black players could not play with white players. It was going to take someone very strong to change the rules.

That person turned out to be Jackie Robinson. He was asked to join a baseball team in New York called the Brooklyn Dodgers. Many fans were angry when they heard a black person was going to play on the team. People wrote him threatening letters. They yelled at him when he was on the field and mocked him. Some of the other players did not want Jackie on their team either. Jackie just kept playing baseball. He did so well during his first season that he was named Rookie of the Year; he hit 12 home runs and stole 29 bases.

During the 10 years Jackie played for the Dodgers, the team won six pennants and played in the World Series.

Jackie stopped playing baseball in 1956. After he left the team, he raised money for the National Association for the Advancement of Colored People (NAACP) and spoke for the rights of black people. Later, Jackie was elected to the Baseball Hall of Fame.

It was what he did with his life that helped African Americans even more than his words. Jackie Robinson broke the color barrier in sports. He showed everyone that a black player could be a winner. By doing this, he opened the sports world for other black players. Thanks to Jackie, everyone has the chance to play ball.

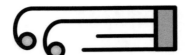

JACKIE ROBINSON
(1919–1972)

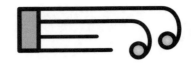

It was clear from the start that Jackie Robinson was great at sports. He went to college at UCLA. He played four sports while he was there. He played baseball, basketball, and football and ran track. He won letters in all of them.

At the time Jackie was growing up, teams were **segregated**. That meant that only white players were allowed to play on the professional teams. Black players could not play with white players. It would take someone very strong to change the rules.

That person was Jackie Robinson. He was asked to join a baseball team in New York called the Brooklyn Dodgers. Many fans were upset that a black person was going to play on the team. People wrote him angry letters. They yelled at him when he was on the field. Some of the other players did not want Jackie on their team either. Jackie kept playing baseball. He did so well during his first season that he was named Rookie of the Year. He hit 12 home runs and stole 29 bases that year.

Jackie's team won six pennants. The team played in the World Series. All of this happened during the 10 years that Jackie played with the team.

Jackie stopped playing baseball in 1956. He raised money for the National Association for the Advancement of Colored People (NAACP). He spoke about the rights of black people. Later, Jackie was given a place in the Baseball Hall of Fame.

What he did in his life helped black people even more than his words. Jackie Robinson broke the color barrier in sports. He showed everyone that a black player could be a winner. He opened the sports world for other black players. Thanks to Jackie, everyone has the chance to play ball.

JACKIE ROBINSON
(1919–1972)

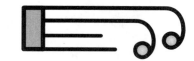

1. Choose a good title for this story.

   A. Breaking the Color Barrier in Sports

   B. A Great Baseball Player

   C. Jackie Robinson's College Years

   D. How Jackie Stole Second Base

2. What does the word **segregated** mean in the story?

   A. forced to play together

   B. chopped into pieces

   C. kept apart by race

   D. mixed together

3. Number the following events in the order they happened.

   _____ Jackie speaks about equal rights for black people.

   _____ Jackie is elected to the Baseball Hall of Fame.

   _____ Jackie joins the Brooklyn Dodgers.

   _____ Jackie wins letters in four sports in college.

   _____ Jackie's team wins six pennants.

4. Answer the following questions.

   • What award did Jackie win during his first year with the Dodgers?

   _____

   • What group did Jackie help raise money for?

   _____

   • Where did Jackie go to college?

   _____

   • How did Jackie show people that African Americans can be great at sports?

   _____

   _____

5. Why was Jackie's baseball career important?

   A. He was the first black player to play on a professional team.

   B. He was the first person to win an award during his first year on a team.

   C. He was the first person to steal bases in baseball.

   D. He was the first person elected to the Baseball Hall of Fame.

BONUS: What do you think it was like to be the first black player on a professional baseball team? Imagine that you are Jackie Robinson. Write a paragraph about how you think you would feel on your first day playing for the Brooklyn Dodgers.

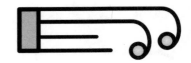

ALEX HALEY
(1921–1992)

A grandmother talked about her family while a little boy named Alex Haley listened to her stories. She told Alex that long ago a young man had been stolen from Africa. He came to the United States on a ship. He was sold as a slave.

Alex grew up, and when he was 18 years old, he joined the Coast Guard. World War II had started. Alex was a good writer, so he helped other sailors write love letters to their girlfriends! He also started to write stories of his own. He sent them to magazines to try to get them published, but nobody liked them enough to buy them.

After the war, Alex worked as a journalist, writing articles for magazines. One day, he was working at a library. He found the names of his great-grandparents in a **record** there, which made him start thinking about his grandmother's stories again.

Alex thought he could find out more about his family. He knew it would be hard. Black people had trouble tracing their family trees.

Slaves were counted like animals, not like human beings. Sometimes, their names were never written down.

Alex had clues. He had some words that his ancestor, Kunta Kinte, had brought with him from Africa. After a lot of hard work, Alex found Kunta Kinte's tribe. He learned many other things about his family, as well. He wrote about all of his discoveries in a book called *Roots*. Alex's book also tells the story of the wrongs of slavery.

People loved *Roots*. It made them want to find out about their own families. The book was made into a miniseries for TV. Millions of people have watched it.

Alex wrote other books. But, *Roots* is the one that everyone remembers. Later, some people said that Alex copied parts of *Roots* from another book. No one is sure if that happened. But, the book gave hope to many African American people that they, too, could find out about their families' pasts.

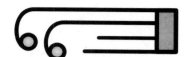 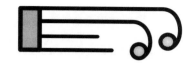

ALEX HALEY
(1921–1992)

A grandmother talked about her family. A little boy named Alex Haley listened to her stories. She told Alex that long ago a young man had been stolen from Africa. He came to the United States on a ship. He was sold as a slave.

Alex grew up. When he was 18 years old, he joined the Coast Guard. World War II had started. Alex was a good writer. He helped other sailors write love letters to their girlfriends! He also started writing stories of his own. He sent them to magazines to try to get them published. But, nobody liked them enough to buy them.

Alex wrote stories for magazines after the war ended. One day, he was working at a library. He found the names of some of his family members in a **record** there. He started thinking about his grandmother's stories again.

Alex thought he could find out more about his family. He knew it would be hard. Black people had trouble following their family trees. Slaves were counted like animals, not like people. Sometimes, their names were never written down.

Alex had clues. He had some words that his first ancestor, Kunta Kinte, had brought with him from Africa. Alex worked very hard. He found Kunta Kinte's tribe. He learned other things about his family, too. He wrote a book about it called *Roots*. Alex's book also tells the story of the wrongs of slavery.

People loved *Roots*. It made them want to find out about their own families. The book was made into a show for TV. Millions of people have watched it.

Alex wrote other books. But, *Roots* is the one that everyone remembers. Later, some people said that Alex copied parts of *Roots* from another book. No one is sure if that happened. But, the book gave hope to many black people that they, too, could find out about their families' pasts.

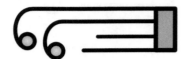

ALEX HALEY
(1921–1992)

1. This story tells about:

   A. a man who fought in a war.

   B. a man who had a grandmother.

   C. a writer who learned about his family and wrote a book about it.

   D. a man who found where his family came from in Europe.

2. What does the word **record** mean in the story?

   A. a piece of music

   B. something put in writing and saved

   C. a kind of video camera

   D. a place where something crashed

3. Number the following events in the order they happened.

   ____ Alex writes love letters for sailors during the war.

   ____ Alex writes a book about his family history.

   ____ Alex's story is put on TV.

   ____ Alex listens to his grandmother's stories about a young African man.

   ____ Alex finds Kunta Kinte's tribe in Africa.

4. Answer the following questions.

   • What is the name of Alex's book about his family history?

   _____

   • Who first told Alex about his family history?

   _____

   • When did Alex serve in the Coast Guard?

   _____

   • What clues did Alex have to help him find his tribe in Africa?

   _____

   _____

   _____

5. Why did Alex think it would be hard to learn about his family's past?

   A. His family had been slaves, and there were not good records of slaves.

   B. His family did not talk about themselves very much.

   C. Alex was an orphan and didn't know any stories about his family.

   D. Alex did not care very much about his family's past.

BONUS: What is one story you know about your family's history? Write it down.

SHIRLEY CHISHOLM
(1924–2005)

Shirley Chisholm's parents both emigrated from other countries. But, Shirley was born in Brooklyn, New York. Her parents were poor. When she was small, her parents could not afford to take care of her and had to send her to the island of Barbados. She lived there with her grandmother. Her grandmother raised her very strictly and sent her to good schools. Shirley came home to the United States when she was 11. Later, she attended college, earned two degrees, and became a teacher.

Shirley said that she wanted to be a "fighter" like the three women she admired most: her grandmother, Harriet Tubman, and First Lady Eleanor Roosevelt. Shirley met the First Lady when she was 14 years old. Mrs. Roosevelt told her, "You are black, and you are a young woman. But, don't let anybody stand in your way." Shirley never forgot that advice. She was 40 years old when she chose to pursue politics.

First, Shirley was elected to the New York State Assembly, the state's legislature. Then, she ran for Congress. She was the first black woman to be **elected** to Congress.

Shirley thought Congress moved too slowly. She wanted to get votes faster because she had so many people she wanted to help. She once said that she was always fighting to get help for the poor, to end the war in Vietnam, and to get equal rights for women.

Shirley tried to run for president in 1972. She told people that she was not a candidate for blacks or for women. She said, "I am the candidate of the people." She meant that she would fight for all people. She also once said that 36 men had run for president up until that point, and she felt she was easily as good as all but about six of them!

Shirley did not get to run for president. But, she served in Congress until 1983. Then, she went back to teaching. She taught at colleges in Massachusetts and in Georgia. They were both women's colleges. Shirley also wrote two books. Her life showed what a black woman could do if she did not let people stand in her way.

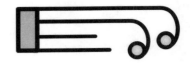

SHIRLEY CHISHOLM
(1924–2005)

Shirley Chisholm was born in Brooklyn, New York. Her parents both came from other countries. They were very poor. Shirley was sent to live with her grandmother when she was a little girl. Her grandmother lived on an island called Barbados. Shirley's grandmother was very strict. She sent Shirley to good schools. Shirley was 11 when she came back to New York. Later, she went to college. She earned two degrees. Then, she became a teacher.

Shirley said that she wanted to be a "fighter." She wanted to be like three strong, amazing women. One was her grandmother. One was Harriet Tubman. One was First Lady Eleanor Roosevelt. Shirley met the First Lady when she was 14 years old. Mrs. Roosevelt said, "You are black, and you are a young woman. But, don't let anybody stand in your way." Shirley never forgot those words. She was 40 years old when she chose to run for office.

First, Shirley was **elected** to the New York State Assembly. Then, she ran for Congress.

Shirley was the first black woman to be elected to Congress.

Shirley thought Congress was too slow. She wanted to get faster help for people. She once said that she was always fighting. She fought to get help for the poor. She wanted to end the war in Vietnam. And, she fought for the rights of women.

Shirley tried to run for president in 1972. She told people that she was not running for blacks. She said that she was not running for women. She said, "I am the candidate of the people." She also said that 36 men had run for president before 1972. She said that she was as good as all but about six of them!

Shirley did not get to run for president. But, she served in Congress until 1983. Then, she went back to teaching. She taught at two colleges. Shirley also wrote two books. Her life showed what a black woman could do if she did not let people stand in her way.

NAME: _____ DATE: _____

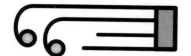

SHIRLEY CHISHOLM
(1924–2005)

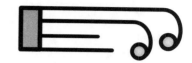

1. Choose a good title for this story:

   A. The Woman Who Ran for President

   B. Life in Barbados

   C. Getting Something Done

   D. A Fighter in Congress

2. What does the word **elected** mean in the story?

   A. chosen by the voters

   B. filled with electricity

   C. appointed by a president

   D. sent to another place

3. Number the following events in the order they happened.

   _____ Shirley starts working as a teacher.

   _____ Shirley meets Eleanor Roosevelt.

   _____ Shirley becomes a member of Congress.

   _____ Shirley goes to live with her grandmother.

   _____ Shirley tries to run for president.

4. Answer the following questions.

   • What was Shirley's first job?

   _____

   • Who told Shirley not to let anybody stand in her way?

   _____

   • What did Shirley fight for in Congress?

   _____

   _____

   • When did Shirley try to run for president?

   _____

5. Why was Shirley's election to Congress important?

   A. She was the first woman to be elected to Congress.

   B. She went to work for the First Lady.

   C. She was the first black person to be elected to Congress.

   D. She was the first black woman to be elected to Congress.

BONUS: Is there somebody in your life who helps you stand up for yourself? Who is that person? Write a paragraph that describes the person and how he or she helps you.

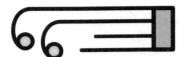

ANDREW FOSTER
(1925–1987)

The boy had been very ill. One day, he woke up in the hospital. The whole world was silent. He could no longer hear.

Andrew Foster was 11 years old when he became **deaf**. After that, he could not go to his regular school. Instead, he had to go to a special school for children who were hearing impaired. Andrew worked hard. When he was 17 years old, his family moved to Detroit, Michigan. Andrew went to work in a factory. He became a war worker, making equipment to help soldiers in World War II.

At that time, there was a college in Washington, D.C., for deaf students. Andrew tried many times to enroll there. The school finally accepted him. Andrew graduated in 1954. He was the first black student to earn a degree there. He studied to be a teacher.

Andrew wanted to help other deaf people, and he decided to go to Africa. In Africa at that time, people hid children if they could not hear, pretending that the children did not even exist. Andrew wanted to change that. He wanted to show that people with hearing problems are smart, can learn, and can work at good jobs.

Andrew started in the country of Ghana. He established a school there. He found 50 deaf children to start in his classes. After only a few years, the school had 100 students, and 300 more were waiting to get in. Andrew turned over his school to other teachers. He moved to another country, Nigeria. He started over.

In each country, Andrew set up classes, schoolrooms, and camps for deaf children. He helped older students get accepted to colleges in the United States. He went to the United States every year, too. He raised money there and then went back to Africa to start another school.

Andrew Foster started 31 schools for deaf students in Africa. In 1987, he died in a plane crash. He was flying from one school to another at the time of his death. His schools still help thousands of children in Africa. His hard work led them to learning.

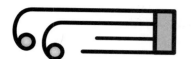
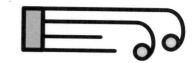

ANDREW FOSTER
(1925–1987)

The boy had been very ill. He woke up in the hospital. The whole world was silent. He could no longer hear.

Andrew Foster was 11 years old when he became **deaf**. After that, he could not go to his regular school. He had to go to a school for children who could not hear. Andrew worked hard. When he was 17 years old, his family moved to Detroit, Michigan. Andrew went to work in a factory. He became a war worker. He made things to help soldiers in World War II.

At that time, there was a college for deaf students. It was in Washington, D.C. Andrew tried many times to go to school there. The school said yes at last. Andrew finished college in 1954. He was the first black student to get a degree at the school. He planned to be a teacher.

Andrew wanted to help other deaf people. He chose to go to Africa. At that time, people in Africa hid deaf children. They pretended that the children did not exist. Andrew wanted to change that. He wanted to show that people with hearing problems are smart. They can learn. They can work at good jobs.

Andrew started in the country of Ghana. He created a school there. He found 50 deaf children. They started in his classes. Soon, the school had 100 students. There were 300 more students waiting to get in. Andrew turned over his school to other teachers. He moved to another country. He started over.

In each country, Andrew set up classes. He started camps for deaf children. He helped older students go to colleges in the United States. He went to the United States every year, too. He raised money there. Then, he would go back to Africa to start another school.

Andrew Foster started 31 schools for deaf students in Africa. He was flying from one school to another when he died in a plane crash. But, his schools still help thousands of children in Africa. His hard work led them to learning.

ANDREW FOSTER
(1925–1987)

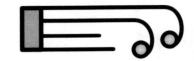

1. This story tells about:

   A. what it is like to be deaf.

   B. how one deaf man helped thousands of children.

   C. how people once treated deaf children in Africa.

   D. how hard it once was for deaf students to go to school.

2. What does the word **deaf** mean in the story?

   A. not able to see

   B. not able to learn

   C. not able to walk

   D. not able to hear

3. Number the following events in the order they happened.

   _____ Andrew becomes ill and loses his hearing.

   _____ Andrew goes to college in Washington, D.C.

   _____ Andrew dies in a plane crash.

   _____ Andrew works in a factory during World War II.

   _____ Andrew raises money to start schools in Africa.

4. Answer the following questions.

   • When did Andrew Foster become deaf?

   _____

   • Whom did Andrew want to help?

   _____

   • When did Andrew finish college?

   _____

   • In what country did Andrew start his first school?

   _____

5. Why do you think Andrew wanted to go to Africa to help deaf children?

   A. Deaf children were treated very badly in Africa.

   B. He wanted to show people in Africa that deaf students could learn.

   C. He wanted to help Africans with hearing problems get degrees and jobs.

   D. all of the above

BONUS: Choose one of your senses—hearing, sight, taste, touch, or smell. Write a list of all of the things you know about because of that one sense.

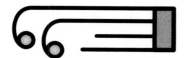
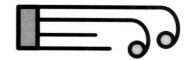

MARTIN LUTHER KING, JR.
(1929–1968)

The Reverend Dr. Martin Luther King, Jr., was born into a family of ministers. His grandfather and father both led the same church in Atlanta, Georgia. Martin decided he, too, wanted to become a minister. He went to school, and when he graduated, he became the minister of a church in Montgomery, Alabama.

Martin worked at his church and also started working for the National Association for the Advancement of Colored People (NAACP). Then, everything changed. Rosa Parks was arrested in 1955. She would not give her bus seat to a white man. Martin was chosen to lead black people in a boycott. The bus boycott in Montgomery lasted for 382 days, and while it was happening, Martin was in danger. His house was bombed, and he was arrested. Many people were angry with him, but he kept going until the Supreme Court forced the buses to change their rules.

After that, Martin started traveling around the country. Whenever something happened that was unfair to black people, Martin was there. He spoke and led peaceful protests. He did not think it was right to hurt other people or destroy things to show strong feelings.

In 1963, Martin helped plan a big rally in Washington, D.C. It was called the March on Washington. Over 250,000 people went to Washington to ask the president and Congress to make the laws fair for all people. The people gathered at the Washington Mall. They listened to speeches, and Martin's speech was the most powerful of all. People still listen to this speech today. He talked about his dream that white people and black people could live together in **harmony**.

Martin's dream did not come true during his lifetime. He kept working to help people. He went to Memphis, Tennessee, in 1968 because some workers there were on strike. He wanted to help them. He was standing outside of his hotel room when a white man shot and killed him. But, Martin's brave words and inspiring ideas are still alive. Americans honor him every year on the third Monday of January, Martin Luther King Day.

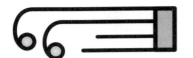

MARTIN LUTHER KING, JR.
(1929–1968)

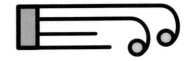

The Reverend Martin Luther King, Jr., was born into a family of ministers. His father was a minister in Atlanta, Georgia. His grandfather was a minister in the same church. Martin chose to be a minister, too. He went to school. When he finished school, he led a church. The church was in Montgomery, Alabama.

Martin worked at his church. He also joined the National Association for the Advancement of Colored People (NAACP). Then, Rosa Parks was arrested in 1955. She would not give her bus seat to a white man. Martin was chosen to help. He led the black people of the city in a boycott. The bus boycott in Montgomery lasted for 382 days. While this was going on, Martin was in danger. His house was bombed. He was taken to jail. Many people were angry with him. But, he kept going until the Supreme Court made the buses change their rules.

After this, Martin started taking trips around the country. When something happened that was unfair to black people, Martin was there. He spoke. He led peaceful marches and meetings. He did not think it was right to hurt other people or break things to show strong feelings.

In 1963, Martin helped plan a big rally in Washington, D.C. It was called the March on Washington. Over 250,000 people went to the capital. They were asking for fair laws for all people. This huge group of people gathered at the Washington Mall. They heard speeches. Martin gave the most powerful speech of all. People still listen to this speech today. He talked about his dream. He dreamed that white people and black people could live together in **harmony**.

Martin's dream did not come true during his life. He kept working to help people. He went to Memphis, Tennessee, in 1968. Some workers there were on strike. He wanted to help them. He was standing outside of his hotel room when a white man shot and killed him. But, Martin's brave words and inspiring ideas are still alive. Americans honor him every year on the third Monday of January. That is Martin Luther King Day.

NAME: _____   DATE: _____

 # MARTIN LUTHER KING, JR.
(1929–1968)

1. Which of the following best describes Martin Luther King, Jr.?

   A. friendly

   B. brave

   C. greedy

   D. tired

2. What does the word **harmony** mean in the story?

   A. trouble

   B. singing

   C. peace

   D. hurt

3. Number the following events in the order they happened.

   _____ Martin speaks during the March on Washington.

   _____ Martin leads a church in Montgomery.

   _____ Martin goes to Memphis to help workers on strike.

   _____ Martin leads the bus boycott.

   _____ Martin lives with his family in Atlanta.

4. Answer the following questions in complete sentences.

   • When is the holiday to remember Martin Luther King, Jr.?

   _____

   _____

   • Who did Martin try to help in Memphis?

   _____

   • In what year did the March on Washington take place?

   _____

   • How did Martin Luther King, Jr., die?

   _____

5. Why do you think we still honor Martin Luther King, Jr.?

   A. He was a brave leader.

   B. He helped African Americans.

   C. He worked all of his life to help other people.

   D. all of the above

BONUS: Write a paragraph about what the world would be like if everyone could live together in peace.

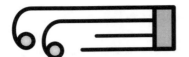

FAITH RINGGOLD
(1930– _____)

 aith Ringgold was born in Harlem, New York. She lived with her mother, who was good at many things, including sewing. Faith wanted to paint. She went to college to study art, and she started painting pictures. Her mother told her she should try making dolls, too. So, Faith made some dolls, and her mother sewed outfits for them. It was not until 1980 that Faith chose to make her first quilt, which she did with her mother's help.

Historically, black women have made quilts for many reasons. They sewed quilts to keep warm, to make things that were bright and colorful, and even to create secret maps to help slaves escape. Faith wanted to make quilts that tell stories. Some of her quilts show her family and her childhood, and some show stories of characters Faith created. In 1988, Faith made a quilt called "Tar Beach." It shows a little girl who lived in Harlem in the 1930s. In the quilt, the girl is shown with her family, spending an evening on the roof of their apartment building—their "tar beach."

Someone suggested that Faith should turn the story from her quilt into a book for children, and she agreed. She wrote the story of a little girl, Cassie, and she painted pictures of Cassie to go with her story quilt. After that, Faith kept writing children's books. She wrote a story about Rosa Parks, a book called *Dinner at Aunt Connie's House*, and a book about Martin Luther King, Jr., among others.

Today, Faith still makes her story quilts, and she still writes books. She works in a **studio**, a special, large room where she can make her art. She built this place for herself in New Jersey. She is living her dream of being an artist. As she wrote in one of her books, "Every good thing starts with a dream."

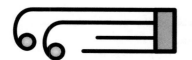

FAITH RINGGOLD
(1930– ____)

Faith Ringgold was born in Harlem, New York. Her mother was good at many things, including sewing. Then, Faith wanted to paint. She went to college to study art. Faith started painting pictures. Her mother told her she should try making dolls, too. Faith made some dolls, and her mother sewed outfits for them. It was not until 1980 that Faith chose to make her first quilt. She did this with her mother's help.

Historically, black women have made quilts for many reasons. They sewed quilts to keep warm. They sewed quilts to make things that were bright and colorful. They made quilts that had secret maps to help slaves escape. Faith wanted to make quilts that tell stories. Some of her quilts show her family and her childhood. Some of them show stories of other people. In 1988, Faith made a quilt called "Tar Beach." It shows a little girl who lived in Harlem in the 1930s. She and her family are spending an evening on the roof of their apartment building—their "tar beach."

Someone suggested that Faith should turn the story from her quilt into a book for children. Faith agreed. She wrote the story of a little girl, Cassie. She painted pictures of Cassie to go with the story quilt. After that, Faith kept writing children's books. She wrote a story about Rosa Parks. She wrote a book called *Dinner at Aunt Connie's House*. She also wrote a book about Martin Luther King, Jr.

Today, Faith still makes her story quilts. She also writes books. She works in a **studio**, a special, large room where she can make her art. She built this place for herself in New Jersey. She is living her dream of being an artist. As she wrote in one of her books, "Every good thing starts with a dream."

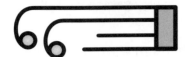
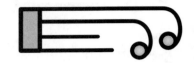

FAITH RINGGOLD
(1930– ____)

1. What is the main idea of the third paragraph?

   A. Faith started making quilts.

   B. Faith made paintings and dolls.

   C. Faith turned one of her children's books into a story quilt.

   D. Faith started to write children's books after turning the story from one of her quilts into a book.

2. What does the word **studio** mean in the story?

   A. a type of house where a person can live

   B. a place where an artist works

   C. a place where a scientist works

   D. a type of studying

3. Number the following events in the order they happened.

   ____ Faith makes a quilt called "Tar Beach."

   ____ Faith writes a story about Rosa Parks.

   ____ Faith starts creating paintings.

   ____ Faith writes her first children's book.

   ____ Faith goes to college to study art.

4. Answer the following questions.

   • What kind of art did Faith make first?

   _____

   _____

   • Who is one well-known person about whom Faith wrote a book?

   _____

   • When did Faith make her first quilt?

   _____

   • How did Faith's mother help her with her art?

   _____

5. Why did Faith write her first children's book?

   A. Someone said that she should turn the story from her quilt into a book for children.

   B. She liked children and wanted to stop making art.

   C. She always wanted to be a writer.

   D. She wanted to help children.

BONUS: Think of a picture you might like to draw that shows your family. Write about it. What time of year is it? What is your family doing? Why is this special?

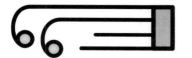

ALVIN AILEY
(1931–1989)

The boy sat in the dark theater. One by one, the dancers came onto the stage. The boy watched them leap, spin, and glide. They were telling a story through dance. It was the most important and memorable moment of the boy's life.

The boy was Alvin Ailey. He grew up in Texas. When his father left the family, he picked cotton with his mother to make money. When he was a young child, Alvin liked to paint and draw, and his mother thought he might grow up to be an artist. He also had a gift for learning languages. He and his mother moved to Los Angeles, California. When he was in junior high school, Alvin's class went to see a **ballet** by a Russian dance company. It was the first time Alvin saw dance onstage.

After that breakthrough moment, Alvin tried to see as much dance as he could. He traveled downtown to go to theaters and meet dancers. He visited the school of a famous dance instructor named Lester Horton. Alvin sat and watched the classes for six months before he was brave enough to join them.

Lester Horton was one of the few teachers who worked with students of different races. He had a dance company that was integrated, and Alvin was asked to join. Then, Lester Horton died suddenly in 1953. Alvin, who was only 23, became the head of the company. He created dances for the company to perform. He chose the music and the stories for each dance.

Alvin decided to move to New York. He danced in shows on Broadway and was given dancing parts in movies. He kept creating dances and started his own dance company. By 1958, Alvin had created a series of dances called *Blues Suite*, a work that became a big hit. His company was famous.

Alvin set dances to music that came from black history. He used folk songs and jazz. He also used other kinds of music, such as classical pieces. He wanted his dancers to show that they could create dances that told a variety of stories. But most of all, he wanted to honor the history of African Americans through his dances. The theater for dance that he started is still open today, and the dancers still honor him and the history of the black community with their work.

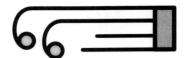

ALVIN AILEY
(1931–1989)

The boy sat in the dark theater. One by one, the dancers came onto the stage. The boy watched them leap, spin, and glide. They were telling a story through dance. It was the most important moment of the boy's life.

The boy was Alvin Ailey. He grew up in Texas. When his father left the family, he and his mother picked cotton to make money. When he was a young child, Alvin liked to paint and draw. He was also good at learning languages. He and his mother moved to Los Angeles, California. When he was in junior high school, Alvin's class went to see a **ballet**. It was the first time Alvin saw dance onstage.

After that, Alvin tried to see as much dance as he could. He went downtown to go to theaters and meet dancers. He visited the school of a famous dancer named Lester Horton. Alvin sat and watched the classes for six months before he was brave enough to join them.

Lester Horton was one of the few teachers who worked with students of different races. He had a dance company, and Alvin was asked to join. Then, Lester Horton died in 1953. Alvin became the head of the company. He was only 23. He created dances for the company to perform. He chose the music and the stories for each dance.

Alvin moved to New York. He danced in shows on Broadway. He was given dancing parts in movies. He kept creating dances and started his own dance company. By 1958, Alvin had created a series of dances called *Blues Suite*. It was a big hit. His company was famous.

Alvin set dances to music that came from black history. He used folk songs. He used jazz. He also used other kinds of music. He wanted his dancers to show that they could create dances that told a variety of stories. But most of all, he wanted to honor the history of African Americans. The theater for dance that he started is still open today. The dancers still honor him and the history of the black community with their work.

ALVIN AILEY
(1931–1989)

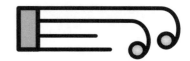

1. Which of the following best describes Alvin Ailey?

   A. large

   B. handsome

   C. wild

   D. creative

2. What does the word **ballet** mean in the story?

   A. a type of dance that tells a story

   B. a type of sport where players hit a ball

   C. a show with lots of singing

   D. a type of dance that is free-form

3. Number the following events in the order they happened.

   _____ Alvin and his mother move to Los Angeles.

   _____ Alvin becomes the head of a dance company.

   _____ Alvin sees a ballet for the first time.

   _____ Alvin is given dancing parts in movies.

   _____ Alvin's father leaves the family.

4. Answer the following questions.

   • What did Alvin do as a child to help his mother make money?

   _____

   _____

   • Who gave Alvin a place in his dance company?

   _____

   • In what year did Alvin finish *Blues Suite*?

   _____

   • How did Alvin become the head of a dance company?

   _____

   _____

   _____

5. Why did Alvin use folk songs and jazz for some of his dances?

   A. He liked the way the music sounded.

   B. He wanted to use new music for his dancers.

   C. He wanted to honor black history.

   D. He did not like other kinds of music.

BONUS: Think of a song you know that tells a story. What is the story about? How could it be made into a dance? Write a paragraph about it.

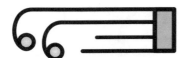

COLIN POWELL
(1937– _____)

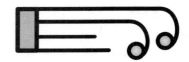

Colin Powell grew up in the South Bronx of New York, New York. He was an average student in school and was not good at sports. He was not sure what he wanted to do when he grew up. When Colin Powell first went to college, he decided he wanted to learn about rocks, so he studied geology. Then, he joined the Reserve Officers Training Corps (ROTC) in college. This is a group that trains people to be officers in the military while they are still students. That's when Colin found what he wanted to do. He wanted to join the United States Army.

Colin was sent to fight in the Vietnam War. He was in a helicopter crash in 1968 and was badly hurt. But even with his injuries, he still helped other soldiers escape from the burning wreckage. He was given the Soldier's Medal for this act. He earned a total of 11 medals while he was fighting in Vietnam.

After the war, Colin went back to school to get a master's degree and then went to work at the White House. He served in both Korea and in Germany, but many of his jobs were based in Washington, D.C. He became the Chairman of the Joint Chiefs of Staff, the chief advisor to the president on military matters and the highest position in the Defense Department. Colin was the youngest person to hold this job. This position was given to him by President George H. W. Bush.

In 2001, President George W. Bush **appointed** Colin Powell to be Secretary of State. This important job meant that Colin traveled around the world, meeting with world leaders. He was the first black person to have this job, which he held until 2005.

Since retiring from government work, Colin Powell has also helped create and run several organizations. One of these organizations is called America's Promise, a group that helps young people who have not had many opportunities in their lives. It offers them improved chances for learning and helps them become better students.

Colin Powell has achieved many firsts in African American history and has made an important impact in America.

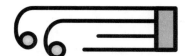

COLIN POWELL
(1937– _____)

Colin Powell grew up in the South Bronx of New York, New York. He was an average student in school. He was not good at sports. He was not sure what he wanted to do when he grew up. When Colin Powell first went to college, he wanted to learn about rocks. So, he studied geology. Then, he joined the Reserve Officers Training Corps (ROTC), in college. This is a group that trains people to be officers in the military while they are still students. Colin had found what he wanted to do. He wanted to join the United States Army.

Colin was sent to fight in the Vietnam War. He was in a helicopter crash in 1968. He was hurt badly. But, he still helped other soldiers. He helped them get out of the wreck. He was given a Soldier's Medal for this act. He earned 11 medals during the war.

After the war, Colin went back to school. He earned a master's degree. Then, he went to work at the White House. He also served in Korea and in Germany. But, many of his jobs were in Washington, D.C. He became the Chairman of the Joint Chiefs of Staff. In this job, he was the main person to advise the president about the military. Colin was the youngest person to hold this job. It was given to him by President George H. W. Bush.

In 2001, Colin Powell became the Secretary of State. He was **appointed** by President George W. Bush. This was an important job. It meant that Colin traveled around the world. He met with world leaders. He was the first black person to have this job. He held the job until 2005.

Colin Powell has also helped start and run several groups. One group is called America's Promise. This group helps young people who have not had many chances in their lives. It helps them learn more and become better students.

Colin Powell has achieved many firsts in black history. He has made an important impact in America.

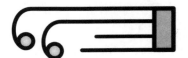

COLIN POWELL
(1937– _____)

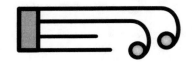

1. What is the main idea of the second paragraph?

   A. how Colin Powell grew up in the South Bronx

   B. how Colin Powell went to work for the White House

   C. what happened to Colin Powell in Vietnam

   D. what Colin Powell does today

2. What does the word **appointed** mean in the story?

   A. to make a doctor's appointment

   B. to point at something

   C. to be fired from a job

   D. to give someone an official job

3. Number the following events in the order they happened.

   _____ Colin is given the job of Chairman of the Joint Chiefs of Staff.

   _____ Colin serves in the war in Vietnam.

   _____ Colin gets his first job at the White House.

   _____ Colin grows up in the South Bronx.

   _____ Colin becomes Secretary of State.

4. Answer the following questions.

   • What group did Colin join in college?

   _____

   • Who appointed Colin to be the Chairman of the Joint Chiefs of Staff?

   _____

   • In what year was Colin hurt in the war in Vietnam?

   _____

   • What is one way Colin has helped young people?

   _____

   _____

   _____

5. Why did Colin earn the Soldier's Medal?

   A. He was hurt in a crash.

   B. He helped other soldiers get out of a helicopter crash even though he was hurt.

   C. He served as a soldier in the war in Vietnam.

   D. none of the above

BONUS: If you could talk to one of the leaders of the world, whom would you talk to and what would you say? Choose the most important thing you would want to say. Write a paragraph about it.

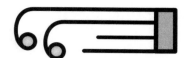
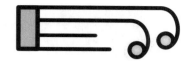

WILMA RUDOLPH
(1940–1994)

As a child, Wilma Rudolph did not look like she would ever be an athlete. She only weighed 4.5 pounds at birth. She was often sick during the first years of her life. After one particularly bad illness, Wilma's parents saw that one of the little girl's legs was weak. This was the first sign that Wilma had **polio**. Polio is an illness that can cripple a person's legs or arms. Wilma's doctor said that Wilma would never be able to walk. But, Wilma never gave up believing that she could beat polio.

The doctor put braces on her legs. Wilma's brothers and sisters had to make sure she kept the braces on. They also helped rub her legs to make them better. Wilma had to go to the hospital every week. She struggled to make her legs stronger. At the age of 9, Wilma took off her leg braces forever.

After strengthening her legs, Wilma decided she wanted to play sports as much as she could. She loved basketball and was a member of her school team for three years before the coach let her play. But, once she had a chance to play, she set a state scoring record. It was in track and field that Wilma would really excel, though. As a sprinter on her high school track team, she was undefeated.

In 1956, Wilma went to the Olympics in Australia to compete in track. She won a bronze medal, which was for third place. Then came the 1960 Olympics in Rome, Italy. Wilma was the shining star, winning three gold medals in track events! She was the first American woman, black or white, to win that many medals in one year at the Olympics.

After she retired from sports, Wilma became a teacher and a coach for other track stars. Wilma also worked for civil rights. Wilma Rudolph never gave up her dreams, even when others said that they were impossible.

African American Achievers

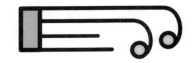

WILMA RUDOLPH
(1940–1994)

Wilma Rudolph did not look like a future athlete as a child. She weighed less than five pounds when she was born. She was also sick many times as a young child. After one bad illness, Wilma's parents saw that one of the little girl's legs was weak. This was the first sign that Wilma had **polio**. Polio can cripple a person's arms or legs. Wilma's doctor said that Wilma would never be able to walk. But, Wilma was not going to give up.

The doctor put braces on her legs. Wilma's brothers and sisters had to make sure she kept the braces on. They helped rub her legs to make them better. Wilma had to go to the hospital every week. She worked hard to make her legs stronger. When she was 9 years old, Wilma took off her leg braces forever.

Once she could walk on her own, Wilma wanted to play sports. She started by playing basketball. She had to work hard to get onto the court. Her coach did not let her play for three years. But, when she started, she set a state scoring record. However, her real skill was in track and field. She won every race as a sprinter on her high school track team.

In 1956, she went to the Olympics in Australia to compete in track. She won a bronze medal. That was for third place. Then came the 1960 Olympics in Rome, Italy. Wilma was the shining star. She won three gold medals in track! She was the first American woman, black or white, to do that in one year at the Olympics.

After she left sports, Wilma became a teacher. She worked as a coach for other track stars. She also worked for equal rights for African Americans. Wilma Rudolph never gave up her dreams, even when others said that they were impossible.

NAME: _____ DATE: _____

WILMA RUDOLPH
(1940–1994)

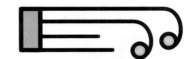

1. What is the main idea of this story?

   A. how Wilma Rudolph overcame polio

   B. how Wilma Rudolph came from a big family

   C. how Wilma Rudolph overcame polio to become a great track star

   D. how Wilma Rudolph was the first American woman to win three gold medals

2. What does the word **polio** mean in the story?

   A. an illness that causes people to lose their hearing

   B. a type of sport

   C. an illness that cripples a person's legs or arms

   D. a way of measuring something

3. Number the following events in the order they happened.

   _____ Wilma's parents take her to a doctor, who says she has polio.

   _____ Wilma sets a state scoring record in basketball.

   _____ Wilma goes to the Olympics in Rome, Italy.

   _____ Wilma takes off her leg braces.

   _____ Wilma weighs less than five pounds when she is born.

4. Answer the following questions.

   • What did Wilma win at the 1956 Olympics?

   _____

   _____

   • Who helped Wilma get better by rubbing her legs?

   _____

   • In what year did Wilma win three gold medals?

   _____

   • What sport did Wilma play after she took off her leg braces?

   _____

5. Why do you think Wilma got better and could walk again?

   A. She worked hard and had lots of help from her family.

   B. She wanted to play basketball.

   C. She wasn't as sick as the doctors thought she was.

   D. She would not go to the hospital every week.

BONUS: Write a poem or a paragraph about running. What does it feel like to run fast? What do you hear? What do you see as you run?

African American Achievers

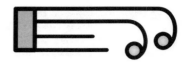

OPRAH WINFREY
(1954– _____)

Oprah Winfrey overcame a hard childhood to make her living in TV. She lived with her grandmother when she was young. Then, she moved in with her mother. She was so unhappy that she ran away when she was 13 years old. The police found her and sent her to live with her father in Nashville, Tennessee. He was strict, making sure she was home early every night. He made her read one book every week and write a report for him about it. That's how Oprah's love of books began.

Oprah's first job in TV was as a reporter, but she was not very good at reporting the news. Reporters are supposed to be calm and detached from the stories they talk about. Oprah would cry if a story was sad and laugh at something funny. So, she was given a job **hosting** a talk show. She was in charge of asking guests questions and running the show. The show was in Baltimore, Maryland. Then, Oprah went to Chicago, Illinois, to do a show there.

Oprah also got a chance to act in some movies, but hosting the talk show was her favorite occupation. Oprah's show was first broadcast across the country in 1986, and people loved it. People still love Oprah's show. Oprah likes to talk to many types of people, and she is easy to talk to. She gives her opinions about many things. Her talk show has won many awards.

In 1996, she announced the beginning of Oprah's Book Club. Thousands of people read the books Oprah talks about on her show and then share their thoughts on her Web site. Because of Oprah's Book Club, reading has become more popular than ever!

Oprah has become very wealthy. She gives away a lot of her money to help people. Oprah gives money to students and to people in Africa. She is starting a school for girls in South Africa and has many other projects to help women, students, and poor people.

Oprah has had an amazing life so far. One reason for her success is that she treats her guests and audience members like friends.

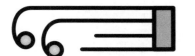

OPRAH WINFREY
(1954– _____)

Oprah Winfrey overcame a hard childhood to make her living in TV. She lived with her grandmother when she was small. Then, she moved in with her mother. She was so unhappy that she ran away when she was 13 years old. The police found her. They sent her to live with her father in Nashville, Tennessee. He was strict. He made sure she was home early every night. He made her read one book every week. Then, she had to write a report about it. That's how her love of books started.

Oprah's first job in TV was as a reporter. She was not very good at reporting the news. Reporters are supposed to be calm. Oprah would cry if a story was sad. She would laugh at something funny. So, she was given a job **hosting** a talk show. She ran the show and asked the guests questions. The show was in Baltimore, Maryland. Then, Oprah went to Chicago, Illinois, to do a show there.

Oprah also got a chance to act in some movies. But, hosting the talk show was her favorite job to do. Oprah's show was first broadcast across the country in 1986. People loved it. People still love Oprah's show. Oprah likes to talk to many types of people. She tells people what she thinks. Her talk show has won many awards.

In 1996, she started Oprah's Book Club. Thousands of people read the books Oprah picks for her book club. Readers can share their thoughts about each book on her Web site. Because of Oprah's Book Club, reading has become more popular than ever!

Oprah has become very rich. She gives away a lot of her money to help people. Oprah gives money to students and people in Africa. She is starting a school for girls in South Africa. She has many projects to help women, students, and poor people.

Oprah has had an amazing life so far. One reason for her success is that she treats her guests and audience members like friends.

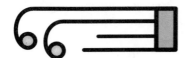 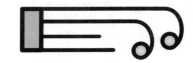

OPRAH WINFREY
(1954– _____)

1. Choose a good title for this story.

   A. The Talk Show Star

   B. A Hard Childhood

   C. How Oprah Helps Students

   D. Oprah and Her Favorite Books

2. What does the word **hosting** mean in the story?

   A. throwing a party

   B. spraying with water

   C. haunting

   D. running a TV show and asking the guests questions

3. Number the following events in the order they happened.

   _____ Oprah runs away from home.

   _____ Oprah wins awards for her talk show.

   _____ Oprah leaves her grandmother's house and lives with her mother.

   _____ Oprah works to open a school for girls in South Africa.

   _____ Oprah is a TV reporter in Nashville.

4. Answer the following questions.

   • What was Oprah's first TV job?

   _____

   _____

   • Who raised Oprah when she was a very young child?

   _____

   • Where was Oprah sent after she ran away from home?

   _____

   • How did Oprah get her own talk show?

   _____

   _____

   _____

5. Why do you think Oprah did not do well as a reporter but does well on her talk show?

   A. She likes to laugh, cry, and be friendly with people.

   B. She is better at being a host than reporting the news.

   C. She isn't able to hide the way she feels.

   D. all of the above

BONUS: What job do you think you would be good at doing? Write a list showing why you would be good at that job.

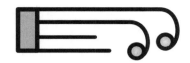

DENZEL WASHINGTON
(1954– _____)

When Denzel Washington was growing up, he didn't think about acting. He liked to write, and he went to college to study journalism. Then, he acted in a play: Shakespeare's *Othello*. He loved it. Next, he acted in a TV movie about the athlete Wilma Rudolph. While he was filming that movie, he met another actor in the cast who later became his wife. After college, Denzel went to San Francisco, California, to enter acting school. The rest of his life seemed to fall into place after that decision.

Denzel finished school and got a part on a TV show. It was about a hospital, and Denzel played one of the doctors. Soon after that, he started receiving offers for parts in movies. In his first big movie, he played a slave who ran away to fight in the Civil War. He won an award in 1989 for his part in that film. He won the Oscar® for Best Actor for a movie he made in 2001 called *Training Day*. He was only the second African American man to win this award.

Denzel has had many different **roles**, playing everything from parts in Shakespeare's plays to leads in action movies. He can play many different parts convincingly.

Denzel's childhood was not easy. His father was a minister who left the family when Denzel was 14 years old. Because his parents got divorced, Denzel feels strongly about family, especially now that he has four children of his own. He says that acting is not his life; his children are his life. He keeps reporters away from his wife and children, but it is clear that his family is close.

Because Denzel feels so strongly about children, he also works to help them. He works for the Boys & Girls Clubs of America. He works for a group called the Children's Fund that helps children in need. He and his wife also work with children at a hospital in Los Angeles, California, and for other charities.

Denzel has acted in and directed many films, but his family continues to be the accomplishment of which he is most proud.

DENZEL WASHINGTON
(1954– _____)

When Denzel Washington was growing up, he didn't think about acting. He liked to write. He went to college to be a journalist. Then, he acted in a play. He loved it. Next, he acted in a TV movie about Wilma Rudolph. He met another actor in the cast who later became his wife. After college, he went to San Francisco, California, to go to acting school. The rest of his life seemed to fall into place after that.

Denzel finished school. He got a part on a TV show. It was about a hospital. Denzel played one of the doctors. Soon after that, he started getting parts in movies. In his first big movie, he played a slave who ran away to fight in the Civil War. He won an award in 1989 for his part in that film. He won the Oscar® for Best Actor for a movie he made in 2001. The movie was called *Training Day*. He was only the second African American man to win this award.

Denzel has had many different **roles**. He has played parts in Shakespeare's plays and in action movies. He can play many different parts well.

Denzel's childhood was not easy. His father was a minister. He left the family when Denzel was 14. Because his parents got divorced, Denzel feels strongly about family. He has four children of his own. He says that acting is not his life; his children are his life. He keeps reporters away from his wife and children. But, it is clear that his family is close.

Because Denzel feels so strongly about children, he also works to help them. He works for the Boys & Girls Clubs of America. He works for a group called the Children's Fund that helps children in need. He and his wife work with children at a hospital in Los Angeles, California. They also help other charities.

Denzel has acted in and directed many films, but his family is still the accomplishment of which he is most proud.

 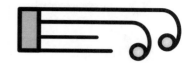

DENZEL WASHINGTON
(1954– _____)

1. What is the main idea of the fifth paragraph?

   A. Denzel works to help children in need because he feels so strongly about his own children.

   B. Denzel does not have time to help other people because of his acting.

   C. Denzel has won awards for his work acting in movies.

   D. Denzel did not go to college; he just went to acting school to be an actor.

2. What does the word **roles** mean in the story?

   A. parts of a story

   B. parts in a movie or a play

   C. parts to fix machines

   D. a type of bread

3. Number the following events in the order they happened.

   _____ Denzel goes to school to study journalism.

   _____ Denzel is in a movie about Wilma Rudolph.

   _____ Denzel's parents get divorced.

   _____ Denzel wins the Oscar® for Best Actor.

   _____ Denzel goes to acting school.

4. Answer the following questions.

   • What does Denzel think is the most important thing in his life?

   _____

   • Who did Denzel meet while he was making his first movie?

   _____

   • In what year did Denzel win his first acting award?

   _____

   • How did Denzel find out he wanted to be an actor?

   _____

   _____

5. Why does Denzel feel so strongly about his family?

   A. He was sad when his parents got divorced.

   B. His wife likes having a close family.

   C. He does not want reporters to bother his family.

   D. He wants to help children around the world.

BONUS: If you could act in a movie, what kind of part would you like to play? Write a paragraph about it.

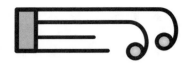

MAE JEMISON
(1956– _____)

When she was a child, Dr. Mae Jemison liked many things. She liked to dance and read. She also liked to look at the stars and loved learning about the planets.

Mae started college when she was only 16 years old. She studied science. She also studied the history of Africa and the history of black people in the United States. Then, she chose a medical school so that she could learn to be a doctor.

Mae became a doctor and went to Africa in 1983. She worked for the Peace Corps, a government group that helps build understanding between America and the rest of the world. She wrote **manuals** to explain how people could take care of health problems themselves. She also cared for patients there. When she came home to the United States, Mae worked as a doctor in Los Angeles, California. But, in 1986, she was given the chance to become an astronaut.

Over 2,000 people applied to be astronauts at the same time Mae did. NASA (the National Aeronautics and Space Administration) only picked 15 people, and Mae was one of them. Mae's big chance to go into space came in 1992. NASA sent a crew to work on a space lab. The team included people from the United States and Japan. In space, Mae did science experiments. She did research about how humans and medicine were affected by space travel. She traveled among the stars she had loved as a child.

Today, Mae enjoys helping students use scientific thinking to try to solve global issues. Mae started a camp where students come together to talk about how to fix world problems. The students are from 12 to 16 years old. They work on these problems for four weeks while they live together. They use science to find possible answers.

Dr. Mae Jemison works to help people understand science and how it affects life every day. Her next big project involves bringing new technology to developing countries.

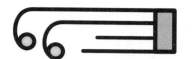

MAE JEMISON
(1956– _____)

When she was a child, Dr. Mae Jemison liked many things. She liked to dance. She liked to read. She also liked to look at the stars. She loved learning about the planets.

Mae started college when she was only 16 years old. She studied science. She also studied the history of Africa. She read about the history of black people in the United States. Then, she went to school to learn to be a doctor.

Mae became a doctor. She went to Africa in 1983. She worked as a doctor in the Peace Corps. The Peace Corps is a government group that helps build understanding between America and the rest of the world. In Africa, she wrote **manuals**. These books told people how to take care of health problems themselves. Then, she came home to the United States. Mae worked as a doctor in Los Angeles, California. But in 1986, she was given a big chance. She was going to be an astronaut.

Over 2,000 people wanted to be astronauts at the same time Mae did. NASA (the National Aeronautics and Space Administration) only picked 15 people. Mae was one of them. Mae's big chance to go into space came in 1992. NASA sent a crew to work on a space lab. The team had people from the United States and Japan. In space, Mae did science experiments. She studied medicines in space. She traveled among the stars she had loved as a child.

Today, Mae likes to help students use science to try to solve global issues. She started a camp. This is a camp where students come together to talk about how to fix problems in the world. The students are from 12 to 16 years old. They work on these problems for four weeks. They live together at the camp while they work. They use science to find answers.

Dr. Mae Jemison helps people understand science and how it affects life every day. Her next big project is bringing new technology to poor countries.

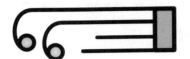

MAE JEMISON
(1956– ____)

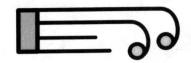

1. What is the main idea of the fifth paragraph?

   A. how Mae worked in space

   B. how Mae was chosen to be an astronaut

   C. how Mae started a camp for students from ages 12 to 16

   D. how Mae learned to be a doctor

2. What does the word **manuals** mean in the story?

   A. by hand

   B. storybooks

   C. books or guides that explain how to do things

   D. a covering to put over books to keep them safe

3. Number the following events in the order they happened.

   ____ Mae becomes a doctor.

   ____ Mae works for the Peace Corps.

   ____ Mae goes into space.

   ____ Mae studies science and African history.

   ____ Mae is chosen to be an astronaut.

4. Answer the following questions.

   • What did Mae like to do as a child?

   _____

   _____

   • Who chose Mae to be an astronaut?

   _____

   • What year did Mae go to Africa?

   _____

   • How does Mae help young people today?

   _____

   _____

5. Why did Mae start her camp for students?

   A. It is part of her work as an astronaut.

   B. It is part of her work to help people understand how important science is.

   C. It is part of her work as a doctor.

   D. none of the above

BONUS: What do you think it would be like to travel into space? Write a story about what it would be like.

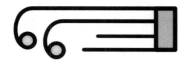 

Benjamin Banneker............... 7

1. D; 2. C; 3. 4, 2, 1, 5, 3; 4. He lived in Maryland; He built a wooden clock with chimes; His work cabin was the place where he mapped the night sky; Pierre L'Enfant was the person who planned Washington, D.C.; 5. B

Elizabeth Freeman 10

1. B; 2. C; 3. 1, 5, 4, 3, 2; 4. He was the lawyer who helped Mum Bett win her freedom; Mum Bett lived in Sheffield, Massachusetts; Massachusetts ended slavery in the state because of her case; She changed her name to show how proud she was to be free; 5. D

Phillis Wheatley 13

1. A; 2. D; 3. 4, 5, 1, 3, 2; 4. She was Phillis Wheatley's owner; She was luckier than many slaves because Mrs. Wheatley treated her like a daughter; "Phillis" was the name of the ship that carried the stolen girl from Africa to Boston; She was the first African American to publish a book of poems; 5. B

David Walker 16

1. C; 2. A; 3. 4, 2, 5, 1, 3; 4. His friends asked him to move to Canada; The name of his book was *Walker's Appeal*; He wrote his first piece about slavery in 1829; He smuggled copies of his book into the South by sewing them into people's clothing; 5. A

Sojourner Truth...................19

1. C; 2. A; 3. 5, 1, 4, 3, 2; 4. He was the slave Isabella was forced to marry; Her book was about her life as a slave; In 1843, she decided to spend her life helping other people; She lived in a small Dutch village in New York; 5. C

Maria Stewart 22

1. B; 2. C; 3. 4, 3, 1, 2, 5; 4. David Walker was Maria's friend and teacher; She and her husband lived in Boston, Massachusetts; She wrote and spoke about education and the rights of African Americans and women; She was left with nothing because some white men stole her husband's money and business; 5. A

Solomon Northup 25

1. A; 2. D; 3. 2, 5, 4, 1, 3; 4. He lived in New York State; He was given the name Platt when he was a slave; He was sold as a slave in 1841; Bass was a white carpenter who helped Solomon send a letter to his family; 5. B

Frederick Douglass 28

1. C; 2. D; 3. 2, 4, 3, 5, 1; 4. The *North Star* was the newspaper Frederick Douglass started; He traveled to the North by train; He ran away in 1838; He met with President Lincoln; 5. B

Harriet Tubman...................31

1. D; 2. A; 3. 5, 2, 1, 4, 3; 4. The Underground Railroad was a secret system of safe houses and friendly people that helped slaves escape to freedom; She worked on the Underground Railroad from 1850 to 1860; The first slaves she went South to help were her sister, nieces, and nephews; She helped the North by spying on the South; 5. B

Robert Smalls 34

1. A; 2. C; 3. 1, 3, 2, 4, 5; 4. He was a slave who worked on the boats and docks of Charleston Harbor; The name of the ship he took was the *Planter*; He lived in Charleston, South Carolina; He took down the Southern flag and put up a white bedsheet in its place; 5. B

Daniel Hale Williams 37

1. A; 2. C; 3. 1, 4, 3, 5, 2; 4. He was the man whose life Dr. Williams saved by operating on his heart; He did not want to make shoes; He went to medical school in Chicago, Illinois; He became famous when he operated on a man's heart and saved his life; 5. C

Booker T. Washington 40

1. A; 2. C; 3. 5, 1, 2, 4, 3; 4. It was the school that Booker T. Washington started; Black people went to the Tuskegee Institute; He heard about a school for black people while working in a mine; A school day at Tuskegee went from 5:00 A.M. to 9:30 P.M. (16.5 hours long); 5. A

George Washington Carver ...43

1. C; 2. B; 3. 4, 5, 3, 2, 1; 4. He taught people about plants; Booker T. Washington started the school where George taught; He believed that farmers in the South needed help; He invented new ways to use these plants; 5. D

Ida B. Wells-Barnett.............46

1. A; 2. B; 3. 4, 3, 5, 1, 2; 4. The Alpha Suffrage Club taught black women about their rights; She sued a railroad; Ida went to England; She marched in the Illinois group between two white friends; 5. A

Mary Church Terrell.............49

1. D; 2. C; 3. 3, 2, 5, 1, 4; 4. She was raised in comfort and luxury; She married a lawyer named Robert Terrell; She was born in Memphis, Tennessee; She fought against separation of the races by writing for newspapers, giving speeches, and writing a book; 5. D

ANSWER KEY

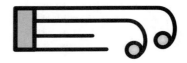

Matthew Henson..............**52**

1. B; 2. C; 3. 2, 3, 1, 4, 5;
4. He was an explorer in Peary's team on all of his attempts to reach the north pole; He was the explorer in charge of the first team to reach the north pole; He got some of his information from the natives; Hundreds of men had died trying to get to the north pole; 5. A

Scott Joplin.....................**55**

1. B; 2. C; 3. 3, 4, 2, 5, 1;
4. He learned to play the banjo first; A German music teacher gave Scott music lessons; The 1893 world's fair was held in Chicago, Illinois; His mother might have asked her employers if he could play their pianos; 5. A

W. E. B. DuBois................**58**

1. D; 2. C; 3. 2, 4, 5, 1, 3;
4. The National Association for the Advancement of Colored People—it is a group that helps black people in the United States; The NAACP was started in 1909; His first students were 30 children attending a corncrib school in the country; They were having the most trouble in the South; 5. A

Bessie Coleman.................**61**

1. C; 2. A; 3. 4, 1, 2, 5, 3;
4. Her childhood was difficult; He was Bessie's brother in Chicago with whom she went to live; She was born in Texas; She started flying as a pilot in the United States in 1922; 5. A

Marian Anderson...............**64**

1. C; 2. C; 3. 2, 3, 1, 5, 4;
4. She was famous for her singing; Eleanor Roosevelt helped her plan an outdoor concert; The concert in Washington, D.C., was held at the Lincoln Memorial; Answers will vary but may include: She gave prize money she won to help black music students; 5. C

Louis Armstrong................**67**

1. D; 2. A; 3. 5, 2, 4, 3, 1;
4. He played jazz; He was the band leader who gave Louis a job in his band; He was born in New Orleans, Louisiana; He acted in 30 movies; 5. D

Langston Hughes...............**70**

1. B; 2. C; 3. 1, 2, 5, 4, 3;
4. He wanted Langston to build buildings and bridges; His class-mates in the eighth grade voted him "Class Poet"; Harlem is a section of New York City; He used the beat of the music in his poems; 5. B

Thurgood Marshall.............**73**

1. D; 2. B; 3. 3, 4, 1, 2, 5;
4. It is the highest court in the United States; He worked for the NAACP; He could have gone to Harvard; There were no black Supreme Court justices before Thurgood Marshall; 5. D

Jesse Owens.....................**76**

1. D; 2. D; 3. 1, 3, 5, 2, 4;
4. He broke three world records in less than one hour; He was the head of the German government; They were held in Berlin, Germany; He earned money by running, lecturing, and speaking for companies like Ford Motor Company; 5. C

Rosa Parks.......................**79**

1. C; 2. A; 3. 3, 2, 4, 5, 1;
4. She disobeyed a law that gave white bus passengers the right to take the seat of any black passenger; Dr. Martin Luther King, Jr., led the group; She lived in Montgomery, Alabama; The Supreme Court ruled that the laws were wrong; 5. D

Daisy Bates.....................**82**

1. C; 2. C; 3. 2, 5, 1, 4, 3;
4. Her newspaper was called the *Arkansas State Press*; She helped nine black students get into Central High School; They started their newspaper in 1941; She helped black students start going to white schools; 5. A

Gwendolyn Brooks.............**85**

1. C; 2. D; 3. 2, 4, 1, 3, 5;
4. She won the Pulitzer Prize; She wrote about families like her own; She wrote her first poem when she was seven; She wrote her second book of poems in 1949; 5. D

Jacob Lawrence..................**88**

1. A; 2. D; 3. 4, 5, 1, 2, 3; 4. He studied painting and drawing; He painted pictures of Harriet Tubman and Frederick Douglass; He lived in the Harlem section of New York City; He studied life around him, went to museums, and studied black history; 5. A

Jackie Robinson.................**91**

1. A; 2. C; 3. 4, 5, 2, 1, 3;
4. He was named Rookie of the Year; He helped raise money for the NAACP; He went to college at UCLA; He showed that African Americans can be great at sports by becoming a great player on a major league team; 5. A

Alex Haley.......................**94**

1. C; 2. B; 3. 2, 4, 5, 1, 3;
4. His book about his family history is called *Roots*; His grandmother first told him about his family history; He served in the Coast Guard during World War II, joining when he was 18 years old; He had some words that his first ancestor brought with him from Africa and he knew his ancestor's name; 5. A

Shirley Chisholm 97

1. D; 2. A; 3. 3, 2, 4, 1, 5;
4. Her first job was teaching; Eleanor Roosevelt told her not to let anybody stand in her way; She fought for the poor, for women's rights, and to end the Vietnam War; She tried to run for president in 1972; 5. D

Andrew Foster 100

1. B; 2. D; 3. 1, 3, 5, 2, 4;
4. He was 11 years old when he became deaf; He wanted to help other deaf people; He finished college in 1954; He started his first school in Ghana; 5. D

Martin Luther King, Jr. 103

1. B; 2. C; 3. 4, 2, 5, 3, 1;
4. The third Monday of January is the holiday to remember Martin Luther King, Jr.; He was in Memphis to help some workers who were on strike; The March on Washington took place in 1963; He was shot by a white man while standing on his hotel balcony; 5. D

Faith Ringgold 106

1. D; 2. B; 3. 3, 5, 2, 4, 1;
4. She painted pictures first; Rosa Parks and Martin Luther King, Jr., are well-known people she wrote books about; She made her first quilt in 1980; Her mother helped her with the parts of her art that needed sewing; 5. A

Alvin Ailey 109

1. D; 2. A; 3. 2, 4, 3, 5, 1; 4. He and his mother picked cotton; Lester Horton gave Alvin a place in his dance company; He finished *Blues Suite* in 1958; He became head of the company when the previous head died suddenly; 5. C

Colin Powell 112

1. C; 2. D; 3. 4, 2, 3, 1, 5;
4. He joined the ROTC in college; President George H. W. Bush gave him the job of Chairman of the Joint Chiefs of Staff; He was hurt in 1968; He has helped young people through a group called America's Promise; 5. B

Wilma Rudolph 115

1. C; 2. C; 3. 2, 4, 5, 3, 1;
4. She won a bronze medal at the 1956 Olympics; Wilma's brothers and sisters helped her get better; She won three gold medals in 1960; She played basketball; 5. A

Oprah Winfrey 118

1. A; 2. D; 3. 2, 4, 1, 5, 3;
4. Her first job on TV was as a news reporter; She lived with her grandmother as a young child; She was sent to Nashville, Tennessee, to live with her father; She showed too many feelings as a reporter, so they made her a talk show host; 5. D

Denzel Washington 121

1. A; 2. B; 3. 2, 3, 1, 5, 4;
4. He thinks his children are the most important thing in his life; He met his future wife; He won his first acting award in 1989; He acted in a play while in college and loved it; 5. A

Mae Jemison 124

1. C; 2. C; 3. 2, 3, 5, 1, 4;
4. She liked to read, dance, look at the stars, and learn about the planets; NASA chose Mae to be an astronaut; Mae went to Africa in 1983; She started a camp where students talk about how to fix global problems; 5. B

NAME: _____

ASSESSMENT GRID

	MAIN IDEA	READING FOR DETAILS	SEQUENTIAL ORDER	CONTEXT CLUES	DRAWING CONCLUSIONS
Benjamin Banneker					
Elizabeth Freeman					
Phillis Wheatley					
David Walker					
Sojourner Truth					
Maria Stewart					
Solomon Northup					
Frederick Douglass					
Harriet Tubman					
Robert Smalls					
Daniel Hale Williams					
Booker T. Washington					
George Washington Carver					
Ida B. Wells-Barnett					
Mary Church Terrell					
Matthew Henson					
Scott Joplin					
W. E. B. DuBois					
Bessie Coleman					
Marian Anderson					
Louis Armstrong					
Langston Hughes					
Thurgood Marshall					
Jesse Owens					
Rosa Parks					
Daisy Bates					
Gwendolyn Brooks					
Jacob Lawrence					
Jackie Robinson					
Alex Haley					
Shirley Chisholm					
Andrew Foster					
Martin Luther King, Jr.					
Faith Ringgold					
Alvin Ailey					
Colin Powell					
Wilma Rudolph					
Oprah Winfrey					
Denzel Washington					
Mae Jemison					